Rhetorical Dimensions in Criticism

Rhetorical Dimensions in Criticism

DONALD C. BRYANT ——————————————

Louisiana State University Press
Baton Rouge

ISBN 0-8071-0214-8

Library of Congress Catalog Card Number 72-94149

Copyright© 1973 by Louisiana State University Press

All rights reserved

Manufactured in the United States of America

Printed by Halliday Lithograph Corporation,

West Hanover, Massachusetts

Designed by Albert R. Crochet

To Mary
for the
Best of Reasons

Contents

Preface

The six lectures comprising this volume were presented as the Thirty-Eighth Annual Summer Series of the Department of Speech at Louisiana State University in June, 1972. In accord with the established purpose of the series, they were intended for a general rather than a specialized academic audience. The texts appear in the following pages, therefore, with little readjustment of temper, substance, manner, or idiom from the live, forty-five-minute presentations. Beyond some small refinement of language toward a general, reading audience rather than a particular, listening one, the changes I have made for publication consist of the addition of notes, mainly bibliographical, and significant extension of Lectures III and V on Edmund Burke beyond what was possible within the original time limits. The collection takes its title from the second lecture, thereby suggesting, intentionally, interplay among the series of related themes concerning the arts and artifacts of discourse.

Some readers will have observed over a period of a few years that from time to time since the publication in the *Quarterly Journal of Speech* in December, 1953, of my observations on the functions and scope of rhetoric, I have attempted to exhibit symptoms of progression in my thinking on the subject.

I offer the first lecture in this collection as the latest codicil to my rhetorical testament.

The indebtedness one builds up over the years in the scholarly pursuit of such subjects as I treat in these lectures—rhetoric, the rhetorical art, Edmund Burke—must be taken for granted. It cannot be accounted in detail without error and injustice. In the text and notes I have acknowledged explicitly and by implication many of my obligations to students and colleagues, especially at the University of Iowa.

My special and particular thanks, of course, are owing to Professor Waldo W. Braden and his colleagues, whose invitation provided the impetus which one seems to need in order, at any particular time, to focus and refine one's thinking. Not only do I appreciate the honor of that invitation, but Mrs. Bryant and I are happily indebted to Professor and Mrs. Braden and their associates for generous hospitality and delightful entertainment during the week of the lectures.

Striking evidence of Professor Braden's delicacy in graciousness concerns my sixth lecture, "A Concept of Eloquence." Neither when I proposed the subject nor during preparation and presentation of the lecture did I know, alas, that he had prepared and presented a lecture on "Eloquence as a Creative Art" at the University of Texas in March. Professor Braden refrained from any mention of his lecture, and only later did I learn that it had been published in April in *Vital Speeches of the Day* (pp. 398–401). Though embarrassed, I was pleased to discover that he and I were complementing each other in the best of causes.

D. C. B.

Rhetorical Dimensions in Criticism

I

"Rhetoric: Its Functions and Its Scope" *Rediviva*

To discuss the concepts, and especially to use the terms, *rhetoric* and *rhetorical* before a general audience (though learned) is potentially to step off into a pretty soggy morass—there to conjure with confusion, amble in ambiguity, manipulate misconception, fumble with fatuities, and flounder in fluctuation and fluidity. Somewhere in the rosy semantic mist is "Rhetoric, the Harlot of the Arts," selling herself to him who can pay; but somewhere nearby is pretty Dame Rhetoric in her mediaeval gown, open palm extended, and festooned with the gay flowers of language. And ever and everywhere is Samuel Butler's pedagogue-rhetorician who "could not ope/ His mouth but out there flew a trope," and all of whose rules "Teach nothing but to name his tools."[1]

Over the centuries one great trouble with the term *rhetoric* has been that it is used loosely for the art, the artifact, and a quality of discourse; and often the reference of the designation is quite unclear. That problem is less troublesome in the realm of poetry, for there we have a full complement of useful differentiating terms for artist, art, and output:

poet   poetic[s]   poetry

With rhetoric we are in something of a mess. I don't know how

---

[1] *Hudibras*, Part I, Canto I, 11. 81–82, 89–90.

3

to get clear of it; but I'll suggest a parallel triplet for our
present purposes of distinction:

   rhetor   *rhetoric*   *rhetory*

I don't expect it to become very popular; but make what you
can of it—at least for the time being. The situation with *criticism* is hardly better; but I'll try to do something with it in due
course.

I should like to be understood, nevertheless; so without trying to disenfranchise any of the meanings of *rhetoric* and
rhetorical which may be current in learned and popular us-
age, I claim the prerogative of the famous Humpty Dumpty
in *Alice Through the Looking Glass* and declare that for these
lectures and for our common purposes, *rhetoric* means what
I say it means—no more and no less.

And so—when I say "Rhetoric is" or "Rhetorical signifies,"
please understand me to mean, "I am using the word *rhetoric*
as a name for . . ." or "I am using the adjective *rhetorical* to
characterize. . . ." By *rhetoric* I shall not usually mean the
output of speakers, writers, songsters, revolutionary guita-
rists, or mass chanters of "Right on" and "We shall overcome," though all of that output, I should readily agree, may
be rhetorical. It may be rhetory in the new triplet. I shall
admit that in its most unrestricted sense rhetoric may signify
those principles, theories, laws, hypotheses, and other stata-
ble propositions which govern and explain the making and
the functioning of symbolic communicative efforts through
which men direct and control each other's beliefs, convictions,
and behavior. That will be the most comprehensive meaning
within which I shall move. I shall wish to confine that meaning, however, in certain traditional ways—for this present
context, at least.

Consequential changes are abroad in the means and
phenomena of instrumental communication in our society,
and in the needs and resources for understanding them. Im-

pressive new efforts are being made to refine and strengthen old methods and to develop new ones for achieving enlarged understanding and consequent measures of control. I shall direct attention to some of them as we proceed. First, however, I would review certain elements of the relevant past in order to interpret the title I have given this lecture: "Rhetoric: Its Functions and Its Scope, *Rediviva.*"

Two decades ago, Bower Aly, then the editor of the *Quarterly Journal of Speech,* invited me to write for that journal a piece which should delineate for the general academic reader essential characteristics, extent, functions, and limits for rhetoric as a field of study as it had been redeveloped in the first half of this century. No comprehensive, characterizing statement had been published for thirty years—that is, since Hoyt H. Hudson's "The Field of Rhetoric" of 1923,[2] early in the new era. The appreciable maturing of the study during the intervening three decades seemed to call for a fresh view.

Nine years before the appearance of Hudson's essay a small group identifying itself as Academic Teachers of Public Speaking had separated from the organized teachers of English and from the "elocutionists," in order, the secessionists thought, more freely and profitably to pursue, revive, and redevelop in Academia Americana the principles, teaching, practice, and theory of oral discourse, especially public address.

Soon, around the original seventeen "academic teachers of public speaking" who founded a national association and created a professional organ, the *Quarterly Journal of Public Speaking,* clustered more and more dissidents of similar or

[2]Hoyt H. Hudson, "The Field of Rhetoric," *Quarterly Journal of Speech Education,* IX (1923), 167-80; reprinted in Raymond F. Howes (ed.), *Historical Studies of Rhetoric and Rhetoricians* (Ithaca: Cornell University Press, 1961), 3-15.

associated interests—teachers of argumentation from departments of English, debate coaches, sponsors of dramatic clubs and directors of academic theater, speech correctionists of clinical and scientific bent, phoneticians and those successors of the late elocutionists, the professors of oratory and of the oral interpretation of literature. By the time of the publication of Hudson's essay, a broader term than public speaking was required for this enlarged academic tent. The organization had become the National Association of Teachers of Speech and the official publication, the *Quarterly Journal of Speech Education*. The principal pedagogical and scholarly preoccupation of most of the members, however, remained public address—the teaching of speechmaking for use in the contemporary public context, and the revival and remastery of the Western inheritance of rhetorical theory and principles from Corax and Tisias, Plato and Aristotle, Cicero and Quintilian, Wilson and Blair, to Whately, J. Q. Adams, and their successors (in the forefront of whom was James A. Winans).

This tradition, long a staple of Western culture—with ups and downs to be sure—had gone into one of its downs in the nineteenth century. The Boylston Professorship of Rhetoric and Oratory at Harvard had gradually been reformed into the professorship of English literature, and the teaching of public address for public life had become the teaching of English composition for the writing of essays mainly literary in their mode and matter. To this transformation may be credited the building of departments of English preoccupied with the teaching of composition in the schools and colleges and establishment of a literacy of the pen in the educated population of America.

That was a fitting and salutary development, for which we of this century should have no regrets. With it, however, came a reduction of the field of rhetoric—on the one hand to the techniques of sentence and paragraph, of word and figure, in the service chiefly of written composition, and on the other hand to the art of delivery, "elocution," mainly for purposes of literary interpretation and the oratory of scholastic competition and exhibition.

Hence when the professors of public address of Hudson's day sought once again to retrieve the whole art of discourse —the inventional and argumentative rhetoric of Aristotle and Cicero—they found it necessary to reassert the province of their study and their teaching. They needed to reestablish it as the theory and principles of useful public discourse. They needed, also, to redistinguish it from poetics and the fine art of imaginative writing. That distinction and that definition constituted the burden of Hudson's essay and of the other and perhaps more influential contribution two years later by Herbert A. Wichelns, "The Literary Criticism of Oratory."[3]

In the thirty years between Hudson's essay and mine, much happened to rhetoric and to the scope of the field of speech. Not only did public speaking develop a new and prolific pedagogy and a healthy scholarship—first, perhaps, at Cornell and then in the state universities of the Middlewest—but other denizens of the tent flourished like the farms and groves of the Imperial Valley: students and teachers of drama and theater, of phonetics and pronunciation, of speech correction and speech science, of the oral interpretation of literature, of group discussion and group methods, of general semantics and the sciences of communication, of the pedagogy of classroom and curriculum. With the growth of diverse interests grew diverse scholarship and a search for separate identities; and the National Association of Teachers of Speech became

---

[3] Herbert A. Wichelns, "The Literary Criticism of Oratory," in Alexander M. Drummond (ed.), *Studies in Rhetoric and Public Speaking in Honor of James Albert Winans* (New York: Century Co., 1925), 181–216; reprinted in Donald C. Bryant (ed.), *The Rhetorical Idiom* (Ithaca: Cornell University Press, 1958), 5–42.

the Speech Association of America; the journal, the *Quarterly Journal of Speech*, to be joined by *Speech Monographs* (a journal of research) and *The Speech Teacher* (a journal directed primarily to the schools).

By then, of necessity, attempts were being made to redescribe the confederated field of speech, to find a satisfactory statement of the common ground of a province where residents of the several parishes, though mutually sympathetic (usually), were coming more and more to bear the relationship of laymen to each other. In this atmosphere the editor of the *Quarterly Journal of Speech* undertook to commission a series of longish articles on some of the principal substantive areas of instruction, theory, and scholarship served by the journal. These articles were to be acceptable to specialists within the several areas, to be sure; but primarily they were to present to specialists in other areas, or generalists (in effect, laymen), as comprehensive and contemporary expositions as possible of the hallmarks and basic characteristics of the several provinces as they appeared to the professionals within them. At least four such articles appeared, of which mine was the last —"Rhetoric: Its Functions and Its Scope."[4]

I offer this extended tale of the generation of that article in order to account for the particular bias and idiom of it and to show why it is what it is and is not other things which one coming to it afresh might expect. I do not propose to review the drift of the argument. That would be too much like the ordinary course of our pedagogy. Some readers may know it already, or at least have heard of it and have heard some of it contested. Others may be enticed into taking it up for light bedtime reading!

Of course I would moderate and modify portions of that statement if I might. I would mitigate the special pleading

[4] Donald C. Bryant, "Rhetoric: Its Functions and Its Scope," *Quarterly Journal of Speech*, XXXIX (1953), 401–24.

which was a function of the time, I might damp a tendency to pontification and self assurance, and perhaps I would obscure some visible touches of neo-Aristotelian myopia. For what it is and for what it was intended to be, however, I still think it a fair, defensible, and serviceable statement.

Apparently I read pretty well the mind and temper of our disciplines at the time. The essay, so to speak, hit the teachers and doctrinaries in speech and English "between wind and water." Perhaps, as Burke said of Charles Townshend, it seemed to lead because it was so sure to follow.[5] At any rate, it has been anthologized six or eight times in the two decades and seems destined for another appearance or two. In the burgeoning field of graduate study in rhetoric, "Functions and Scope" joined the orthodox canon as a "classic" essay; and later it came to serve as a staple, conservative explication of rhetoric for the makers of anthologies and writers of articles among those new rediscoverers of rhetorical concepts, the students of English composition. I cannot feel displeased—for myself or for the study and teaching of discourse.

Though I would not recall that statement of 1953 even if I might, or recant any of its major tenets, I welcome this opportunity to review it publicly in the light of the education I have enjoyed for the past two decades, especially from my associates, both students and colleagues, at the University of Iowa. Those have been the decades of rapid acceleration of "new" rhetorics—Kenneth Burke's and I. A. Richards' of course (already mellowed into subjects of doctoral dissertations) and Richard Weaver's; but especially the explosive concepts of Marshall McLuhan on the one hand, and on the other the philosophical explorations into rhetoric and the rhetorical explorations into philosophy led by Chaim Perelman, Henry Johnstone, and the journal *Philosophy and Rhetoric.* During

---

[5] Edmund Burke, *Speech on American Taxation,* in *The Works of the Right Honorable Edmund Burke* (12 vols.; Boston: Little, Brown, 1894), II, 64–65.

those same decades behavioral-quantitative studies in communication have achieved a certain maturity which reinforces the impossibility of ever viewing things rhetorical again, either substantively or methodologically, precisely as we could in 1953. So it is; but not to all eyes are prominent features of the rhetorical world of 1973 invisible in that of 1953, or the principal propositions of 1953 irrelevant to 1973.

Perhaps it is presumptuous, or at least premature, to refurbish and in a sense to relaunch my notions of the function and scope of rhetoric until the essays and commentaries deriving from the recent National Developmental Project in Rhetoric and published in its report have had time to infiltrate the classrooms, the seminars, the dissertations, and the learned studies of the rhetorical scholars of the seventies. If so, perhaps I may meliorate the presumption or haste by confessing at once that with many of the prominent concepts promulgated by the conferees I find it congenial to associate mine. Their "ruling objective," for example, is stated in terms with which I am altogether comfortable:

> to develop an outlined conception of rhetoric applicable to our own time. We conceived of rhetoric in the classical, and richest, sense—as the theory of investigation, decision, and communication concerned particularly with practical, especially civic, affairs. Our central aims, then, were to revitalize a humanistic discipline whose theory and literature are exceptionally rich, and to attempt redefinition and perfection of that discipline as a modern method of problem-solving and decision-making.[6]

The sources and forces for discovery and redevelopment are many and vigorous. So far as they are humanistic and humane their results will be salutary. So far as they are focused and embodied in the yield from the National Developmental

---

[6] Lloyd F. Bitzer and Edwin Black (eds.), *The Prospect of Rhetoric: Report of the National Developmental Project* (Englewood Cliffs, N.J.: Prentice-Hall, 1971), 237.

Project, they may be uncertain; but they are striving, as I see it, in the proper arena.

Let us turn, then, to some important features of the doctrine of two decades ago to see how it should be different, and how the same, were I now proposing it for the first time.

No doubt it would now be well to alter, or at least to qualify, the working definition of rhetoric as it then appeared. "First of all and primarily," I wrote, "I take rhetoric to be *the rationale of informative and suasory discourse.* All its other meanings are partial or morally-colored derivatives from that primary meaning." I still find that definition defensible and operationally viable. At the same time I recognize that it may be interpreted as setting arbitrary limits to the scope in one respect and opening it up too much in another. That definition has been questioned on two grounds: first, for the inclusion of "informative" with "suasory" and second for the limitation to "discourse."

Edwin Black, for example, found the coupling of informative and suasory "open to question" because "informative discourse is not usually associated with rhetoric, either historically or at present. . . . In the tradition that can be traced from Plato and Aristotle through Campbell in the eighteenth century and Whately in the nineteenth to Kenneth Burke in our own time, only two major writers on rhetoric have involved informative as well as persuasive discourse in their definitions of rhetoric: Quintilian and Campbell."[7] And, Black argues, neither really meant to include the informative as a clearly separate genre. As a matter of fact, I think, neither did I. At least, now I do not; and now I modify the wording of the definition accordingly in order to put the focus on the functions or dimensions of discourse rather than the genres.

[7] Edwin Black, *Rhetorical Criticism: A Study in Method* (New York: Macmillan, 1965), 11–12.

Black's historical argument serves his immediate purposes well enough, no doubt, but it would seem to require for validity a special definition of *informative* which somehow excludes the instructional or illuminative. Such a limitation has certainly been obsolete at least since the eighteenth century.[8] If, however, one wished to counter Black's argument historically, one might cite the three ends of oratory reiterated in Roman rhetoric—*docere, delectare, movere* (teach, please, and move)—and the strong implication, at least in principle if not in operational doctrine, that any of the three could be the dominant purpose in a particular rhetorical work. When *docere* is the dominant purpose, the genre informative is potential. It is not necessarily created, of course, unless we have some analytic use for it; and genre criticism at best has limited usefulness. Even if we apply to the ancient ends of discourse the linear adjunct interpretation, as Black does to Campbell's "enlighten the understanding, please the imagination, move the passions, and influence the will," the case against informative discourse within the province of rhetoric is far from conclusive. Let us suppose that Campbell did consider rhetorical discourse generically persuasive, and that the first three ends were rhetorical only as cumulatively they serve to influence the will. Still Campbell cannot have held so unrealistic a notion of individual discourses as not to admit that a particular discourse may serve primarily the end of enlightening the understanding.

[8] See, for example, Wilbur Samuel Howell, *Eighteenth-Century British Logic and Rhetoric* (Princeton: Princeton University Press, 1971), 496–97, 510–11; or Gerard A. Hauser, "Empiricism, Description, and the New Rhetoric," *Philosophy and Rhetoric*, V (Winter, 1972), 24–44. As a contemporary witness may I cite Douglas Ehninger: "A rhetoric I define as an organized, consistent, coherent way of talking about practical discourse in any of its forms or modes. By practical discourse I mean discourse, written or oral, that seeks to inform, evaluate, or persuade, and therefore is to be distinguished from discourse that seeks to please, elevate, or depict." Ehninger, "On Systems of Rhetoric," *Philosophy and Rhetoric*, I (1968), 131.

Historically biased as I may be, however, and as neo-Aristotelian as Black and my essay may label me, I cannot accept as conclusive the argument from silence—I cannot agree that the absence of explicit recognition of the informative as a kind in the rhetorical tradition is permanently confining. Prevailing and developing uses of discourse invite the discovery or formulation of adequate rationales appropriate to them. If for reasons of tradition those rationales may not be conceived as rhetorics, they must be developed nevertheless. James L. Kinneavy, for example, has recently undertaken to develop comprehensive rationales of discourse.[9] Deriving his model from the now-hackneyed communication triangle, Kinneavy arrives at four categories discriminated according to aim: reference discourse, persuasive discourse, literary discourse, and expressive discourse. For each he delineates defining concepts and operational features in massive detail. For persuasive discourse the rhetorical inheritance furnishes the chief substance, and the literary draws upon poetics and criticism from Aristotle to M. H. Abrams—as one might expect. Reference discourse (trifurcated into scientific, informative, and exploratory) and expressive discourse do not emerge sharply or, to me, convincingly. Kinneavy's effort, however, may serve at least to remind some of us that our concepts of rhetoric and poetic may not be altogether adequate to account for all discourse that we are likely to encounter in our time. Whether we adapt to changing modes by making rhetoric more capacious as Kenneth Burke does, or by assigning new names and new concepts to subrationales, may be matters of convenience or of the capacities of our instruments. I cannot now see it as involving theoretic imperatives.

Considering rhetoric, as I do, to comprehend the theory, principles, and technology of instrumental, "advisory" com-

[9] James L. Kinneavy, *A Theory of Discourse: The Aims of Discourse* (Englewood Cliffs: Prentice-Hall, 1971).

munication, functioning first of all but by no means exclusively in practical, public discourse, perhaps it would be well to avoid, without denying, the operationally doubtful difference between informative discourse and suasory discourse. The informative and the suasory as kinds are hard to disentangle with firm assurance except in the textbooks and classrooms of English composition and speechmaking. Earlier it had seemed important to counteract and correct the common assumption that discourse whose principal service is enlightenment—and which is, therefore, not explicitly either persuasive or fictive—is outside the bounds of any systematic theory or rationale of critical analysis except the logical, the grammatical, or the syntactical. That corrective is now, perhaps, hardly necessary. If so, I should be content with the stipulation that the principles of informative discourse (at least so far as the discourse is addressed to the lay audience) are subsumed under the suasory, as they appear to have been in antiquity. Or I might settle for the concept of informative-suasory as all-one-word, or for the double concept sublimated into the term *communicative.* That term, however, popular though it now is through academic associations and departments, and comprehensive and capacious enough to encompass most social activity, comes pretty close, I think, to defeating valid discriminations.

For the foregoing considerations, and for others which I shall develop a little later, I would now define rhetoric as *the rationale of the informative and suasory in discourse.* That wording implies two distinguishable but closely entangled dimensions of discourse as rhetorical, and it implies others which are not. Perhaps it dodges or circumvents the problems of genre, but I think rather that it recognizes pure genres as fictions and implies that most artifacts of discourse exhibit various dimensions, the informative-suasory of which comprise the province of rhetoric. The new wording also removes the obstacle, which I never intended, to admitting the rhetorical into literary analysis.

A second major difficulty critics have found with my original definition is not removed or mitigated by the revision just presented. It is the objection, not to enlarging the scope of rhetoric, but to confining it to discourse. In the former essay, after asserting the seemingly incontestable notion that gold and guns, though frequently effective in controlling behavior, are not in their nature rhetorical, I continued:

> No more shall we admit the persuasive use of all symbols as belonging to rhetoric. Undoubtedly the persuasive force of pictures, colors, designs, non-language sounds such as fog horns and fire alarms and all such devices of symbolic significance is great and useful. . . . Their use has a kinship to rhetoric, and when they are organized in a matrix of discourse, they become what Aristotle called extrinsic or nonartistic means of persuasion. . . . Unless we are to claim practically all interhuman activity as the field of rhetoric, however, some limits must be admitted, even within the field of persuasion. . . . [Hence] I am assuming the traditional limitation to discourse.

For what I think adequate reasons I still choose to treat rhetoric as concerned primarily with discourse—with the web of words. I would not, however, be finicky or arbitrary about how many words in what form qualify as discourse, as long as there are informative or suasory dimensions to their use. Hence I would have no significant trouble with Kenneth Burke's idea of the basic function of rhetoric as "the use of words by human agents to form attitudes or to induce actions in other agents."[10]

When the concept of rhetoric is enlarged, as it now tends to be, to include all symbolic behavior, the enlargement certainly brings out significant kinships among principles operating in the various symbolic systems. Recognition of those

[10] Kenneth Burke, *A Rhetoric of Motives* (New York: Prentice-Hall, 1950), 41.

kinships, to be sure, may convince us that the primary genus we seek to account for is larger than we had permitted ourselves to suppose. To deny the kinships, remote though some of them may seem, and to ignore the enlarged genus, is blindness. To assign *rhetoric* as the most fitting term or concept for the comprehensive genus seems to me to commit an unnecessary offense against useful terminology. It is to force and distort relationships by detaching the designation from a major species and making it serve for a genus which it has not characterized except, perhaps, metaphorically—the "silent rhetoric of thine eye," for example. Bowers and Ochs' definition in *The Rhetoric of Agitation and Control* enlarges the genus about as far as it can go: "the rationale of instrumental symbolic behavior."[11] That definition permits the authors, under the rubric "the Rhetoric of," to combine generically the "symbolic behavior" of pelting policemen with feces, lying down in front of army buses, editorializing in the Chicago *Tribune*, and toasting the Chinese hosts in the Great Hall of the People. There may be theoretic or operational gain from joining together such diverse phenomena and seeking comprehensive principles to illuminate them. Those principles, however, may need to be stated so broadly and vaguely as to be unserviceable for the illumination or generation of constructive distinctions. Bowers and Ochs succeed well in composing a rationale for the basically nonverbal (certainly nondiscourse) behavior which their definitions of agitation and control characterize. The analogical relationships of that rationale to rationales of suasory discourse may be illuminating in both directions; and I would have them and others like them pursued with all the enterprise and ingenuity that may be brought to bear. If it requires the special sanction of the label *rhetoric*, therefore, to make that pursuit viable, or to

[11] John Waite Bowers and Donovan J. Ochs, *The Rhetoric of Agitation and Control* (Reading, Mass.: Addison-Wesley, 1971), 2.

channel it effectively, the gains, I suppose, could be worth the terminological blur.

The scope assigned to rhetorical studies by the Committee on the Scope of Rhetoric at the Pheasant Run conference of the National Developmental Project, too, is expansive but not reckless: "Rhetorical studies are properly concerned with the process by which symbols and systems of symbols have [*i.e.,* exert] influence upon beliefs, values, attitudes, and actions, and they embrace all forms of human communication, not exclusively public address nor communication within any one class or cultural group."[12] The Committee on the Advancement and Refinement of Rhetorical Criticism, at the same conference, enlarged the scope of rhetoric even more explicitly, and to my mind recklessly. They declared: "We shall no longer assume that the subject of rhetorical criticism is only discourse or that any critic studying discourse is *ipso facto* a rhetorical critic. The critic becomes rhetorical to the extent that he studies his subject in terms of its suasory potential or persuasive effect." Hence, they declare, rhetoric as a rationale may profitably serve as an important basis for explaining "any human act, process, product, or artifact which . . . may formulate, sustain, or modify attention, perceptions, attitudes, or behavior."[13]

The liberation of the rhetorician from the shackles of inherited concepts and doctrine so that he may view his role in the 1970s with concepts adequate to the 1970s was the assigned mission of the Pheasant Run conferees and their predecessors in the prior phase of the National Developmental Project, the scholars of Wingspread. The mission was to free the rhetorician from the shackles of his inheritance, not, I think, to forbid him access to it. That is a good mission—one to be accepted and pursued. It requires, I think, the adoption of

[12] Bitzer and Black (eds.), *The Prospect of Rhetoric,* 208.
[13] *Ibid.,* 220.

what Wayne Booth calls a "rhetorical stance"[14] in the redevelopment of theory and doctrine for the study and explanation of human interaction and human behavior, and for the improvement of that behavior. That rhetorical stance, however, it seems to me, must be founded in the assumption—none the worse because traditional and conformable to the experience of the centuries—that discourse has been and will be the primary vehicle of instrumental, symbolic behavior and that the central rationale, the mother lode, is the rationale of the informative and suasory—in the web of words. Reconceiving the concept of discourse as vehicles and users of it change has gone on historically and will continue. Hence Karl Wallace can declare that "Rhetoric is . . . primarily an art of discourse" and then find every rhetorician "directly concerned with what goes on when men adjust to one another through their communications." He concludes, "The ultimate data of the rhetorician are the speech and language men use when they believe they are communicating with one another."[15]

And so, with no impulse to confine the understanding and the exploration of how men communicate, for what, according to what principles, through what languages, what symbols, what signs, and what extrasensory vibrations, I confirm and to some degree extend the concept of the earlier essay—that discourse is the most characteristically rhetorical vehicle. All the more do I feel warranted in such limitation in the present context, because, like Wallace, I am considering rhetoric as the foundation of a productive art whose artifacts are formed in a matrix of words.[16]

[14] Wayne Booth, "The Rhetorical Stance," *College Composition and Communication*, XIV (October, 1963), 139–45.
[15] Karl Wallace, "The Fundamentals of Rhetoric," in Bitzer and Black (eds.), *The Prospect of Rhetoric*, 3–4.
[16] There might arise some resolution of the difficulties I have been treating if, knowing that no one universal system is possible, we spoke as Douglas

Further, for 1973 I would add a modest gloss rather than reinterpretation to the most frequently quoted and paraphrased statement of 1953: that, speaking generally, the central rhetorical function is the *"function of adjusting ideas to people and people to ideas."* I understand that some important exception has been taken to that concept, but I don't know what. I would remark, however, the enhanced importance of the concepts and idiom of behavioral science in the study of communication in twenty years, and the permeation of those concepts and that idiom through rhetorical studies. It would be well, therefore, to recognize more explicitly than I did formerly the obvious involvement of rhetorical discourse in affecting action (BEHAVIOR) as well as ideas—involvement with ideas in action. We must think of rhetorical transactions as functioning to modify the features of desired changes of idea and behavior so that the changes seem feasible and attractive in the available circumstances. We must think of them as functioning at the same time to modify the attitudes of people toward change. Implicit in this concept is the assumption, of course, that the rhetorical function includes the reverse of adjustment to change—reinforcement of the acceptability of no change, that is, intensification of acceptance.

For 1973 I should reassert and reinforce my view of 1953, that rhetoric and poetic are and must be closely and complementarily related. That is the view of enlightened neo-Aristotelians, those of us in the now disestablished Cornell tradition, salted and savored, of course, by the Chicago critics and the Bairdians of Iowa. It is the view I reasserted in our little Iowa collection of papers on rhetoric and poetic of

---

Ehninger recommends ("On Systems of Rhetoric," Part V), of rhetoric-*s* and rationale-*s*. We might then, if we wished, extend rhetorics beyond discourse and treat of a rhetoric of the film, a rhetoric of the dance, etc., without implying that they are all basically one. With respect to the rhetoric of discourse, I have understood and I do understand the plurality of particular systems as implicit in my definition.

1965:[17] the view of the parallel and interactive operation of rhetorical and poetic processes in many sorts of communicative artifacts and situations. I shall develop those relations more explicitly later. They are among the relations recognized in the modification I have made in my definition of rhetoric: that rhetoric is a contributory rationale, as Aristotle and most major theorists since have known it is, for the explanation of imaginative, fictive literature.

It may be unnecessary to reiterate the concept of rhetoric as a rationale of discourse both written and oral—for reader and listener; but in a context where English and speech are distinct and often competing disciplines and departments, and in a society in which orality through the electronic media has regained and secured its place as a prime mode of public discourse, there is profit in the reemphasis. Like dramatic discourse, rhetorical discourse throughout the ages has been oral but has functioned and does function in writing and print as well. Orality, with its particular and distinctive features, is historically, and also genetically, the prime potential dimension of the rhetorical. The surrogate orality of print, with its built-in limitations, is with us, is necessary, and will continue to be. Sometimes among students of literature, and even of rhetoric, there seems to have been the tacit assumption that speaking should be treated, artistically at least, as a kind of lively but loose and undisciplined stage of writing. Serious, responsible students of language, however, have returned firmly (if they ever really departed) to the position that writing is primarily recorded speech with, of course, its special dimensions. Whether oral utterance precedes writing or writing is preparation for potential speaking has functional but not generic significance.

[17] Donald C. Bryant, "Uses of Rhetoric in Criticism," in Donald C. Bryant (ed.), *Papers in Rhetoric and Poetic* (Iowa City: University of Iowa Press, 1965), 1–14.

Let the discourse be spoken or written, however, the rhetorical function was and is central to the preacher, the teacher, the courtroom lawyer, the labor leader, the politician, the critic. It is central also to the advertiser, the propagandist, the journalist, the salesman, the demagogue (and to the writer or lecturer on the rhetorical art)—not only to the individual saint or fanatic, but to the institutionalized, anonymous agencies for engineering consent. Furthermore, the rhetorical in discourse spans the spectrum from the most commonplace harangue to the greatest literature—that is, to the highest eloquence.

In approaching the close of this supplement or codicil to the statement of my rhetorical views of twenty years ago, let me clear up a minor confusion—whether mine or my critics'— which has arisen from a too neat contrast in too crisp a sentence in "Functions and Scope." There I wrote, "Rhetoric is method, not subject." Out of its context, that is certainly an unfortunate statement. Karl Wallace, in one of his often mentioned articles, has demonstrated that rhetoric has substantive, not methodological content only, that it has its characteristic subject matter, even its special subject matter.[18] That subject matter is the values, the prevailing ethical tenets and moral foundations on the basis of which, and in the context of which, men make decisions in their public or social transactions. This is the sort of subject matter which Aristotle atomizes in perhaps tedious detail in specifying the "goods" in the first book of the *Rhetoric.* With that kind of definition of subject matter one can but agree without protest. I can see that the passage to which my controversial sentence contributes has a sort of double face. The one looks upon something like Wallace's foundation of "good reasons." That is the face of the substance of the art of rhetoric. The other looks upon

[18] Karl Wallace, "The Substance of Rhetoric: Good Reasons," *Quarterly Journal of Speech*, LIX (1963), 239–49.

the subject matter of rhetorical discourse. The sentence in question should serve to distinguish the two. Apparently it doesn't.

At the conclusion of my former essay I identified four distinct but closely related roles for rhetoric. (1) As the systematic formulation and organization of principles for the management of discourse with informative-suasory potential, it is an instrumental discipline. (2) So far as it furnishes theory, principles, and methods for describing and accounting for the informing of ideas and the functioning of language in discourse, it is a critical discipline. (3) As it may furnish method for investigation looking to the nature of meaning and the validity and interrelations of ideas, it is philosophical. (4) And as it identifies and treats significant forces governing the behavior of men in society, it is a social discipline. Of those four, stated somewhat differently, I then devoted most space and attention to the first—the instrumental—as I have done in this retrospect. That, no doubt, is why the new friends of rhetoric in the teaching of English composition have been attracted to the essay. Of the philosophy of rhetoric or rhetoric as philosophy, and of rhetorics as rationales for analysis and criticism of discourse, I said very little explicitly. In fact, that essay, because of its limitations, served in part to prompt one of the early pieces in the new philosophical examination of rhetoric, Maurice Natanson's "The Limits of Rhetoric."[19] That is an important kind of enterprise for which I have only the most modest of equipment and no inclination.

If I were literally presenting my rhetoric *rediviva* in the Latin sense as I understand it—that is, if I were now rebuilding with old materials renewed—it should be evident from what I have said that I should utterly reject little that had formed the old building. I should reshape a good many of the

[19] Maurice Natanson, "The Limits of Rhetoric," *Quarterly Journal of Speech*, XLI (1955), 133–39.

old stones, sand-blast them to clear the grime of antiquity, and rearrange here and there to harmonize the architecture with the new construction arising nearby. To escape from the metaphor: So far as I understand the movement of rhetorical studies over the past two decades—and my continuing education has been in the very good hands of younger rhetoricians and older, of behavioral scientists and philosophers—the basic concepts may need to be adapted and supplemented, but not abandoned. Improvements there surely would be, even within the confines of the purpose of the earlier essay; but those improvements would affect the complexity and sophistication of theories, methods, and doctrines rather than concepts of function and scope.

II

Rhetorical Dimensions in Criticism

If, as earlier I have observed, the terms *rhetoric* and *rhetorical* are slippery and elusive, terms hard to pin down securely, and when pinned down, just as hard to use consistently to signify stable concepts, the term *criticism* is hardly in better case. What is criticism, a critic? What are the critic's functions? his province? his obligations? his output? These are questions to which answers vary widely and sometimes negate each other.

How then may one talk about criticism with some likelihood of being understood as one wishes? First, I should suppose, one will recognize that most such words as *rhetoric* and *criticism* tend to focus rather than prescribe the meaning of the contexts in which they are used. Unless we force them arbitrarily, or come to them rigidly committed to particular definitions, they will not impose meanings on contexts. That is to say, from what I discuss in the name of criticism, one will come to know how I understand the term. He will know whether, in any particular context, I mean discourse about *discourse* or discourse developing a *rationale* of discourse; whether, shall we say, I am thinking of Alexander Pope's *Essay on Shakespeare* or his *Essay on Criticism*; whether I have in mind the latter chapters of Thonssen, Baird, and

24

Braden's *Speech Criticism*[1] or Marie Hochmuth Nichols' piece on Lincoln's first inaugural address.[2] In an anthology of English literary criticism of substantial scope, both of the Pope works would probably be included. In a comparable anthology of rhetorical criticism (if there were one) we could very well find large portions of Aristotle's *Rhetoric* as well as the Nichols essay.

In any case, most of the common notions of criticism seem to involve or to imply some analytical examination of an artifact or artifacts, of some human transaction or transactions, toward the end of comprehension and realization of the potential of object or event. Most notions of criticism extend also to appreciation and on to appraisal or judgment. I assume that when C. Harold King explores and explicates the characteristics and qualities of George Whitefield's preaching and generalizes them into the epithet "Commoner Evangelist,"[3] or "God's Dramatist,"[4] he is exercising the critical function. So is Carroll C. Arnold as he illumines Lord Erskines's courtroom discourse in "Lord Thomas Erskine: Modern Advocate."[5] Criticism is the name for Bernard Weinberg's *The Art of Jean Racine*[6] and for his explications of individual symbolist poems.[7] Marie Nichols was critic as she analyzed G. B.

[1] Lester Thonssen, A. Craig Baird, and Waldo W. Braden, *Speech Criticism* (2nd ed.; New York: Ronald Press, 1970), Parts IV–VI, Chs. 12–19.

[2] Wayland M. Parrish and Marie Hochmuth [Nichols], *American Speeches* (New York: Longmans, Green, 1954), 21–71.

[3] C. Harold King, "George Whitefield: Commoner Evangelist," in Raymond F. Howes (ed.), *Historical Studies of Rhetoric and Rhetoricians* (Ithaca: Cornell University Press, 1961), 253–70.

[4] C. Harold King, "God's Dramatist," in Herbert A. Wichelns *et al.* (eds.), *Studies in Speech and Drama in Honor of Alexander M. Drummond* (Ithaca: Cornell University Press, 1944), 369-92.

[5] Carroll C. Arnold, "Lord Thomas Erskine: Modern Advocate," *Quarterly Journal of Speech*, XLIV (1958), 17–30; reprinted in Howes (ed.), *Historical Studies*, 294–308.

[6] Bernard Weinberg, *The Art of Jean Racine* (Chicago: University of Chicago Press, 1963).

[7] Bernard Weinberg, *The Limits of Symbolism: Studies of Five Modern*

Shaw's speaking.[8] Three various articles in criticism follow each other in a recent issue of the *Quarterly Journal of Speech*—on Harold Pinter's *The Caretaker*, John Donne's *Anniversaries*, and Ralph Waldo Emerson's principles of structure;[9] and from two issues earlier one recognizes criticism in Richard Speer's analysis of Edmund Burke's committee reports on the India question.[10] Let us assume—without trying to exemplify all or most of the ventures in criticism open to the ingenuity of man and without trying to exclude other possibilities—that all analytic, interpretive, particularizing, or generalizing examinations of the arts broadly conceived—individual works, kinds, elements, aspects, and authors—are essays in criticism. What, then, within the genus, shall we treat as rhetorical criticism, or better the rhetorical dimension of criticism, however broad or however limited?

The types, kinds, modes, species into which it has seemed useful to differentiate the total, comprehensive critical operation are various and familiar. One of the most common categorizations, featuring the *forms* of artifacts, is that by genre. Hence we have poetic criticism, dramatic criticism, criticism of fiction, speech criticism, each directed to the examination and illumination of works according to familial features and each proceeding by a few distinctive and many common principles. Almost as frequent are the divisions founded in the

---

French Poets (Chicago: University of Chicago Press, 1966).

[8] Marie Huchmuth Nichols, "George Bernard Shaw: Rhetorician and Public Speaker," Chapter VIII of her *Rhetoric and Criticism* (Baton Rouge: Louisiana State University Press, 1963), 109–29.

[9] Robert P. Murphy, "Non-Verbal Communication and the Overlooked Action in Pinter's *The Caretaker,*" *Quarterly Journal of Speech*, LVIII (February, 1972), 41–47; Emory B. Elliott, Jr., "*Persona* and Parody in Donne's *The Anniversaries,*" *ibid.,* 48–57; Lawrence L. Buell, "Reading Emerson for the Structures: The Coherence of the Essays," *ibid.,* 58–69.

[10] Richard Speer, "The Rhetoric of Burke's Select Committee Reports," *Quarterly Journal of Speech*, LVII (1971), 306–15.

critic's or his age's view of the essential relations of art and nature: classic, neoclassic, romantic, naturalistic, realistic, expressionistic; or those founded in a particular ideological view of man or society, such as Freudian criticism, Marxist criticism, Platonic criticism. For some of us, however, the criticism of discourse, while properly conducted in any of the frames of reference which I have mentioned, recognizes a superior or prior distinction according to function. In very general terms, the distinction I mean is that between the treatment of artifacts as significant primarily for what they *are* and the treatment of them as primarily significant for what they *do*.[11] That is the traditional distinction between literary and rhetorical criticism, between criticism of the fine and of the useful arts. It is the functional distinction underlying Herbert Wichelns' position in "The Literary Criticism of Oratory" of 1925.[12] We are usually satisfied to represent that difference by the concepts poetic and rhetorical. Neither term nowadays seems quite adequate for the functions of criticism which are implied for it, but both are familiar enough and traditional enough to serve as well as any.

Wichelns' essay of 1925 set the major direction of critical thought about speeches and speaking for the succeeding decades even to the edge of this moment. Perhaps it did not introduce the term *rhetorical* criticism into working practice as the counterpart of literary criticism, but it certainly launched the term on a persistent career. That essay, a criticism of criticism and a corrective to prevailing practice, reestablished oratory in parallel status with literature as substance for criticism, and it distinguished a concept of criticism appropriate to each. Wichelns' focus upon the criticism of oratory, upon the generic basis for critical distinction,

---

[11] See below, pp. 35, 42.
[12] See I, note 3, above.

tended to identify rhetoric with speaking, and rhetorical criticism with the criticism of speeches (oratory). The essay thus provided the student of speeches and speaking with a critcism all his own, coordinate with literary criticism, and with a genre, *oratory* (public address), to which that criticism is appropriate. That appears, at least in gross terms, to be Wichelns' emphasis. In its time and context, it was an appropriate concept. The fullest expression of it is probably Thonssen, Baird, and Braden's *Speech Criticism*, whose title, still in the revised edition, features the word *speech* rather than *rhetorical.*

"The Literary Criticism of Oratory" implies the notion of a unified, complete criticism, one of whose principal dimensions is the literary (poetic) and another the rhetorical. In the criticism of his time and earlier, Wichelns saw the literary dominant, and when applied to public address not adequately accounting for the essential nature and functioning of the discourse. For explication of Fielding, Addison, or DeQuincey it would do reasonably well; for Fox, Clay, or Cobden it would miss the point widely; and for Burke, Cicero, or Churchill the yield would be interesting, but would exhibit notable inadequacies of explanation. On the other hand, Wichelns believed rhetorical criticism as he conceived it would not go far in explaining Lamb or even Montaigne, but it would be the only criticism worth applying, say, to Colonel Barré[13] or to the majority of public speakers. For Burke, however, who is part of the immediate scene but transcends it, only the literary and the rhetorical together will be equal to the critical task.

It is worth observing that Wichelns does not seem to think of rhetorical criticism as distinguished by system or method but by point of view. "Rhetorical criticism," he wrote, "lies at

[13] Colonel Isaac Barré was a competent debater allied with Chatham and Shelburne in the Parliaments of George III. See below, IV.

the boundary of politics (in the broadest sense) and literature; its atmosphere is that of public life, its tools are those of literature, its concern is with the ideas of the people as influenced by their leaders."[14] One may not wish to agree that the tools of rhetorical criticism are exclusively those of literature. Rhetorical criticism, however, can go far towards its end with those tools, because they are tools for the analysis and interpretation of the language and structure of discourse. What I read into Wichelns, or perhaps impose upon him, is that rhetorical criticism is to be thought of and pursued as a prime dimension of a comprehensive criticism of discourse. Sometimes—often perhaps—it will be the single or dominant dimension; at other times it will not figure significantly in the shape of criticism; but at all times it is a dimension potentially capable of illumining discourse.

In part for these reasons I have recast my definition of rhetoric to make it the rationale of the informative and suasory *in* discourse; and for these same reasons I have chosen to discuss herein rhetorical dimensions in criticism rather than rhetorical criticism.

The first rhetorical dimension in criticism which I will identify and deal with briefly is in a way the most obvious and least theoretically significant. It derives from the role of the critic as rhetor. In themselves and their working, of course, all critical works—both those advancing doctrine and method and those offering analysis, interpretation, and judgment of particular discourses or classes or phases of discourse—are rhetorical even when they are not patently argumentative. Criticism as incarnated in discourse is directed to enlightening and convincing the consumer—the student or audience of plays, speeches, films, television shows; the reader of novels,

---

[14] Herbert A. Wichelns, "The Literary Criticism of Oratory," in Bryant (ed.), *The Rhetorical Idiom*, 41.

poems, essays, pamphlets, periodical papers—or it is directed
to inflating the ethos of the critic, often to both. Both are
rhetorical functions; both fall within the informative or suasory dimensions of discourse. Lawrence Rosenfield in his useful introduction to the nature of criticism, "The Anatomy of
Critical Discourse,"[15] describes the critic as carrying on a kind
of forensic examination—advocacy or defense. Even when the
procedure and atmosphere of debate and deliberation are not
so explicit as they are in Dryden's *Essay of Dramatic Poesy* or
Fénelon's *Dialogues on Eloquence* or Erasmus' *Ciceronianus;*
even when the form and tone are not so explicitly forensic as
they are in Sidney's *Defense of Poesie;* even then it is plain
that across the spectrum from the puff or the debunking review in the *Times* to T. S. Eliot's *Homage to Dryden*, critical
practice, even what Northrop Frye calls academic criticism,
is not notable for scientific neutrality. I have examined, or at
least sampled, the rhetorical practice of literary critics from
Sidney to Dryden and others in an essay in a volume in honor
of Herbert Wichelns.[16] There a reader may see presented a
rhetorical dimension which needs attention in the interpretation of any essay in criticism, rhetorical or literary. Except for
very few theoretical works, if any, critical discourse is corrective, reformative, evaluative, preservative, revisionist, judi-
cial, but never altogether systematically objective and
philosophically comprehensive. Hence it is always rhetorically adjusted to the circumstances of its time and its author. Its statements of doctrine must be understood as
incorporating emphases and deemphases demanded by the
particular state of the controversy and not altogether by the
inherent nature of the subject. That is, the rhetorical purpose

[15] Lawrence Rosenfield, "The Anatomy of Critical Discourse," *Speech Monographs*, XXXV (1968), 50–69.
[16] Donald C. Bryant, "'A Piece of a Logician': The Critical Essayist as
Rhetorician," in Bryant (ed.), *The Rhetorical Idiom*, 293–314.

of the critic will in part determine the shape of his doctrine at any particular time.

A second and more significant rhetorical dimension of criticism, the examination and explication of discourses in their rhetorical functions, appears to have been of slow and late growth;[17] but rhetorical dimensions in the theory and criticism of poetry have been evident almost from the beginning of the formulation of the art. They came on strong in the Hellenistic, and especially the Horatian, view of the nature and function of poetry. The rhetorical stance is obvious in the *docere* and *delectare*, "preferably both," of the Horatian ends of poetry; it is evident in the preoccupation of poetic doctrine with effect on audience, with adaptation to audience, with creation of characters which harmonize with the preconceptions of audiences and fulfill their expectations. The vocabulary of poetic doctrine was largely derivative from rhetoric well into the eighteenth century. Whatever may have been the practice of the best poets over the centuries from Horace to Pope, the writers about poetry, the accusers of poetry, and its defenders and apologists have seen poetry as instrument[18] and without blush or apology have treated poetry in a rhetorical dimension. That dimension in the criticism of literature

---

[17] The ancient Greeks and Romans indulged very little in analytical-judicial criticism of any kind of discourse. To be sure, Socrates' analysis of the presumed speech of Lysias in the *Phaedrus* is analytical-critical. In a sense, so is Aristophanes' raucous examination of Aeschylus and Euripides in the *Frogs*, and Seneca's selection and analysis in the *Suasoriae* of passages from the famous declaimers. One recalls also the capsule characterizations of Sappho, Demosthenes, and Cicero in the Longinian tractate, and of the early Roman orators in Cicero's *Brutus*. Such examples, however, are conspicuous by their rarity. Rhetoric as the practical art of speaking and writing for public discourse has flourished over the centuries mainly as pedagogy and technology, to guide the learner and equip the maker. It has not commonly supplied rationales for criticism—except, in effect, for schoolboys.

[18] See O. G. Brockett's "Poetry as Instrument" in Donald C. Bryant (ed.), *Papers in Rhetoric and Poetic* (Iowa City: University of Iowa Press, 1965), 15–25.

has always been uncongenial to some writers and critics, and
from the early nineteenth century to our day it has enjoyed
severe ill-repute among literary artists and even many critics
and scholars in academia. Perhaps, however, some adjustment or modification is taking place. It is now plain that many
persons again are ready to avow social missions for literature
and the arts; and literary scholars and critics dare in broad
daylight to speak of rhetoric in literature in a sense very close
to that familiar to students of the rhetoric of public address.
Elsewhere I have analyzed some of those uses of rhetoric in
recent literary criticism,[19] so I shall not take time now to
review my findings. A little later I shall come back briefly to
rhetorical dimensions in the criticism of literature.

For the most part, and until fairly recently, though literary
criticism has had its rhetorical dimension from time to time,
the criticism of public address, as most observers have found,
has been what Wichelns called it, the literary criticism of
oratory. It is true, as Wichelns once remarked in disappointment, that the rhetorical criticism of oratory is slow to develop.

What is lacking in the province of rhetoric today—and the
deficiency is not to the credit of those of us who have been in
the mainstream of the twentieth-century revival of rhetoric
in public address—is any considerable body of sophisticated
rhetorical criticism of public address. The critical activity that
has occurred, along with the historical and theoretical study
of rhetoric and the scientific study of communication, has
failed systematically to apply the accumulated inheritance of
rhetorical theory and principle to the phenomena, the processes, the artifacts of public address; nor has rhetorical criticism ventured into new areas of theory and principle.

To be sure graduate departments of rhetoric and public

[19] *Ibid.*, 1–14.

address for several decades have been cultivating rhetorical criticism with earnest redundancy. The output has been appearing frequently in the national and regional journals in speech and in volumes of *festschriften* now and then. The shelves of our university libraries are liberally stacked with dissertations called "Rhetorical Criticism of Select Speeches [or the Speaking] of. . . ." Some of these have occasionally escaped the worst rigidities of matching text against formula to become nearly what they profess in their titles to be, but even then, I fear, almost in spite of themselves. For the most part our critics have not gone much beyond their forebears, the "new" rhetoricians of the twenties and thirties, as Black and others demonstrate with wry generosity.[20] The collective industry of these critics has worn to bluntness the contours of a neo-Aristotelian die. The activity which rhetorical scholarship has fostered—and at its best it is very good—has not been marked by great surges of imagination and enthusiasm like those which punctuate literary criticism with the insights and the grotesqueries of the new criticism, Chicago Aristotelianism, contextualism, imagism, archetypism, mythism, and so forth. Rhetorical criticism's greatest ventures have been led, provoked, or inspired by Kenneth Burke. That is good. Almost anything new or old—Aristotelian or avant-garde—can arise out of Burke and be reinforced from his books. Even he, however, elusive and unschematic as he is, may be in danger of becoming stereotyped as the proprietor of primary critical conjuring-words such as *identification* and *consubstantial,* and of a *pentadic* cookie-cutter to replace the "five great arts" of ancient lore.

Notable attempts to sketch and to elaborate the essential features and methods of rhetorical criticism, or at least to

---

[20] Edwin Black, *Rhetorical Criticism* (New York: Macmillan, 1965), Ch. II, "The Practice of Rhetorical Criticism."

open up the grounds for various kinds of criticism of public address, are known to students of the subject. I have mentioned some of them, and others will come to mind.[21] It may safely be said, I think, that we have much *about* such criticism —the rhetorical dimension of criticism—but as yet nothing really philosophical and comprehensive, nothing comparable to Northrop Frye's *Anatomy of Criticism*, for example. An inclusive formulation of rhetorical criticism is probably being composed somewhere. When it emerges I should expect it to exhibit features common to all criticism, as I have been implying, and features characteristic and distinguishing of the rhetorical.

First, I would assume that rhetorical criticism, like all criticism, participates directly or indirectly in the formulation of theories and systems of principle which describe and account for not only individual objects, but also genres, modes, and dimensions of the discourse which is its province. As the province of literary criticism is the poetic—the fictive and imaginative, the beautiful, the enduring in poems and prose, the eloquence of public affairs and the pulpit—so rhetorical criticism treats of the illuminative and suasory in speeches and speaking, in pamphlets and pamphleteering, in controversy and debate, in editorials and editorializing, in *Grapes of Wrath* and *Mother Courage* and the vehicles and media to which they belong. Rhetorical criticism, then, is directed (1) to discovering and explicating the elements and form of par-

---

[21] Besides the works by Thonssen-Baird-Braden, Black, Hochmuth-Nichols, and Rosenfield which I have mentioned, useful contributions have been made by Thomas R. Nilsen's wide sampling of essays from *Western Speech* and elsewhere in *Essays on Rhetorical Criticism* (New York: Random House, 1968); Robert L. Scott and Bernard L. Brock's collection, *Methods of Rhetorical Criticism: A Twentieth Century Perspective* (New York: Harper & Row, 1972); and Anthony Hillbruner's paperback *Critical Dimensions: The Art of Public Address Criticism* (New York: Random House, 1966). Scott-Brock and Hillbruner, and of course Thonssen-Baird-Braden, furnish helpful bibliographies.

ticular discourses; (2) to generalizing particular discourses, or
their informative-suasory dimensions, into the wider
phenomena of the rhetorical, especially public address; (3) to
showing how particular discourses participate in families of
didactic and suasory discourse to which they may be related;
and finally (4) to supporting value judgments.

Rhetorical criticism is systematically getting inside transactions of communication to discover and describe their elements, their form, and their dynamics and to explore the
situations, past or present, which generate them and in which
they are essential constituents to be comprehended and
judged.

The foregoing characteristics, of course, may appear in literary criticism as well. In rhetorical criticism, however, the
essential *external* reference of discourse, the context both immediate and antecedent, the suasory potential in the situation, plays an organic part different from the part it plays in
other criticism. Suppose, for the moment, that pure poetry, as
Walter Ong says, is created for contemplation, and pure rhetorical discourse for use.[22] Suppose, as Bernard Weinberg sees
it, that the poetic artifact is to be accounted for within the
universe of the work itself, while the rhetorical artifact is
adequately treated only by exploring also essential factors in
the world outside the work.[23] (*Madame Bovary* to Weinberg is
the poetic—self contained; Voltaire's *Candide*, the rhetorical
or mixed.) Then it seems to follow that the text, so to speak,
the total artifact for rhetorical criticism, includes discourse in
a problematic and apparently alterable situation; the role of
criticism, thus, is to discover and explicate the ways and

[22] Walter J. Ong, "The Province of Rhetoric and Poetic," in Joseph
Schwartz and John A. Rycenga (eds.), *The Province of Rhetoric* (New York:
Ronald Press, 1965), 48–56; reprinted from *The Modern Schoolman*, (January,
1942).

[23] Bernard Weinberg, "Formal Analysis in Poetry and Rhetoric," in Bryant
(ed.), *Papers in Rhetoric and Poetic*, 36–45.

means, and to judge the kind and extent of resolution and balance which the discourse as fashioned was capable of bringing about in that situation.

Lloyd Bitzer casts the familiar elements of the total rhetorical event into terms which give freshened definition to the province of rhetoric in criticism.[24] His paper on the subject has already risen above my "Function and Scope" in the hierarchy of orthodox reading for students of rhetoric. Bitzer describes rhetorical discourse (and, he might agree, the rhetorical dimension in other discourse) as coming into being in real, as contrasted to fantastic or fictive, situations. The rhetorical discourse is generated in a situation involving exigence (tension or urgency) which may be removed. The situation demands a fitting response. So far as the response required is discourse (whether artistic or work-a-day), the situation is rhetorical. Rhetorical discourse comes into being *in* the situation, to *affect* the situation, to *alter* the situation by the evocation of reasons and motives through language. The rhetorical, unlike the poetic, includes the sayer as well as the said, the writer as well as the written; thus rhetorical discourse participates in the situation and alters or reconstitutes reality. If the discourse be fitting, the exigence of the situation is removed, reduced, or changed. Here then is the function of criticism: to know and to show what was and what might have been—how nearly fitting, how far removed. If valuative connotations emerge, so much the better.

Rhetorical criticism, then, is first of all analytical; it discovers how the object is made—the verbal artifact and the whole transaction into which the artifact is introduced as a fitting response to preexistent or emerging conditions. By what methods? By those methods of *analysis* which can yield the fullest account of all elements of the discourse. Rhetorical

[24] Lloyd Bitzer, "The Rhetorical Situation," *Philosophy and Rhetoric*, I (1968), 1–14.

criticism is more distinctive in the questions it asks, the phenomena it selects for observation, and the perspective from which it observes them than in the principles or methods on which it proceeds. Wichelns observed, we will recall, that the tools of rhetorical criticism are those of literary criticism, which may be only another way of saying that the common tools of criticism of linguistic artifacts will serve the ends of the kinds of criticism which employ them. Analytic procedures, for example, for explicating the rhythms of language in Lincoln's second inaugural address will not differ operationally from those applicable to *Paradise Lost;* but they will differ in the evidence they reveal of the functions or potentials of those rhythms—poetically, rhetorically, or rhetorico-poetically. Likewise, consideration of kinds and sources of illustration and allusion, in either literary or rhetorical artifacts, ultimately has as its end description and assessment of potential response from listener or reader. The difference between literary and rhetorical dimensions comes in the kinds of responses which they are primarily capable of eliciting. Are the items potentially experiential or instigative, or does the one reinforce the other? In other words, differences of analytic tools do not in themselves make or distinguish differences of stance and function.

When rhetorical criticism has shown how the object is made in its informative and suasory dimensions (however broadly or narrowly one chooses to conceive the object), when it has isolated and identified all the relevant elements of that object and has examined their interrelations and their potential interactions, and when it has described their form, it will then search into the potential *working* of the object in the situation. Here may arise the question of the critic's dependence on ascertainable, determinable, measurable "effect" on audience, reader, viewer. That matter has generated far more verbiage and heat than, in my opinion, it deserves. I am willing, nevertheless, to get embroiled in the dispute—but not for long.

The identification and measurement of the effects of any discourse can be useful to criticism. Effects imply causes in the situation and hence may show the critic what to search for in the total transaction. Measurement of results may help him define the problems with which the rhetor was coping or might have been coping, or perhaps should have been coping. Determination of results, however, is not a critical but an historical undertaking. Results may be identified and measured without antecedent analysis or even knowledge of the discourse. Criticism is concerned with the ways and means discoverable in the discourse, or in the whole transaction, through which the rhetor touched or left untouched or altered the available sources of response which appeared to inhere in the situation or to be generated by the discourse. The quality of the suasory discourse, therefore, has no necessary relation to measurable results; nor are valuative judgments necessarily to be made on the basis of such measurement. Knowledge of results actually occurring may contribute to understanding the functioning of a work, but results in reality are not in themselves measures of quality, though of course they are partial measures of social, cultural, historical significance.

I might wish to modify the foregoing if, through the working of some infinite, clairvoyant computer, programmed by a host of prophets above space and time, *all* the results, present and future, in heart and head, in action and thought, in friend and foe, in rhetor and audience, in art and nature, in society and culture, could be worked through a thousand-dimensional statistical design and pronounced final and comprehensive. But even then, it seems critically significant to ask, not what the effects of the discourse were, but rather what part the discourse played, what part the discourse might have played because it was what it was, and how its part was played, in the rhetorical transaction.

One who discusses rhetorical criticism (or any criticism, for that matter) even as generally as I have been discussing it, will be expected to say something about the evaluative function—the ultimate assessment and appraisal of artifact and performance, of genres, of speeches and speaking, of suasory discourses and suasory discourse. Value judgment will be an end result of criticism of some discourse, of that worthy to be called rhetorical art. The highest function of criticism, as well as of practical instruction, is enrichment of understanding and enhancement of response. Hence most rhetorical as well as poetic treatises, works of critical theory, are couched in the terms of the excellent product, the criteria of the admirable, the effective, the proper: the ideal tragedy, oration, argument. That is well, but with that position must go the qualification embodied in the following advice to students of the arts, including the rhetorical art: "Certainly you will wish to pass judgment on the works which you are studying, to declare your liking or distaste, your sense of the bad and the better. The function of critical study, however, is to enable you to make such appraisals on the foundation of knowledge of what the thing is which you are preferring or dispraising. Until you know as completely as possible what the thing is, and what it might be, you are not ready to render the judgment of criticism but only the response to experience—sensitive, perceptive, inspired, and valuable as that response may be."

That kind of admonition seems to me much more important for the critic of rhetorical transactions than for the critic of the pure arts. The rhetorical dimensions of criticism, as I have said, are not concerned with objects of pure contemplation, but with phenomena of ideas in action, especially public action. The first questions for rhetorical criticism, therefore, are not how good it is, how much we may legitimately praise or

dispraise it or its creator. It is far more important to know in
the most complete sense what it is, what its significance is, and
how, in the situation, it achieves that significance.

To repeat: The proper *first* goal of criticism is explication
and understanding as fitting supports for appreciation. The
scholarly critic—or so I think him—is not primarily a perceptive companion for the adventure of the soul among masterpieces. It would be better to think of him as the analytic
explicator of the adventures of masterpieces among souls.[25]
Rightly conceived, however, he is primarily the expert in-
structor in the mastery of the object—in the realities of form,
substance, function, and operation of all works of a kind (and
for the rhetorical critic the informative-suasory kind), from
the most run-of-the-mill to the masterpiece.

In the course of these explorations I have sought to stir the
earth anew about the roots of an important kind of approach
to understanding man in society, man striving, man seeking
to cope with his own public destiny within his concept of his
world and how it is constructed and propelled. That approach
is through critical study of man's rhetorical art. As I said
earlier, I do not find it fruitful, even if plausible, to enlarge the
rhetorical to comprehend all symbolic interaction, by whatever vehicle communicated. Nor do I find it fruitful or plausible to extend the rhetorical dimensions to encompass all kinds
of study of all kinds and vehicles of symbolic interaction.

For those reasons I am not pleased with that definition of
subject matter in the Report of the Committee on Rhetorical
Criticism of the National Developmental Project in Rhetoric:
"any human act, process, product, or artifact which, in the

---

[25] Thus do I make free with Anatole France's metaphoric definition of the
good critic as "he who relates the adventures of his own soul among masterpieces." Anatole France, *On Life and Letters*, trans. A. W. Evans, *The Works
of Anatole France in an English Translation*, ed. Frederic Chapman (London
and New York: , 1911), XXIV, vii.

critic's view, may formulate, sustain, or modify attention, perceptions, attitudes or behavior."[26] I cannot accept that as a serious, considered characterization of the subject. I can accept it, however, for what I think it was intended to be—a rhetorical extravagance serving to provoke fresh consideration of the rhetorical impulse as it manifests itself in contemporary American society.

Before leaving the subject of criticism, I shall mention some specific developments which I find encouraging and certainly worth exploiting further. One is the emancipation of scholarship in rhetoric from confinement to oral discourse and to discourse which was oral in origin. More and more critics are treating discourse where they find it. Some of us, even in departments of "speech" before they became departments of "communication," have never felt inhibited from studying critically Milton's *Second Defense*, Swift's *Conduct of the Allies*, Burke's *Reflections*, Tom Paine's *Rights of Man*, or the *Federalist Papers*. And we have assumed that in so doing we were rhetorical critics. We have always been liable, of course, to the admonition, "Stick to your speeches." The trouble is that too few others have bothered to do what James T. Boulton, professor of English at Nottingham, has tried recently— to treat non-oral public address "rhetorically."[27] Some critics are now working at it with advancing skills.[28]

[26] Lloyd F. Bitzer and Edwin Black (eds.), *The Prospect of Rhetoric: Report of the National Developmental Project* (Englewood Cliffs, N.J.: Prentice-Hall, 1971), 220.

[27] James T. Boulton, *The Language of Politics in the Age of Wilkes and Burke* (Toronto: University of Toronto Press, 1963), in which Boulton studies rhetorically—though avoiding the term—such works as *The Letters of Junius*, Dr. Johnson's *False Alarm* and *Falkland's Island*, Burke's *Present Discontents* and *Reflections*, and Paine's *Rights of Man*.

[28] We have made significant progress in critical outlook and sophistication since Wilbur Gilman's pioneering formulaic study of Milton's pamphlets, *Milton's Rhetoric: Studies in his Defense of Liberty*, University of Missouri Studies, XIV (Columbia, Mo., 1939), *n.* 3, but there is distance still to travel. Perhaps I illustrate some of the pitfalls in V, below.

Rhetorical dimensions are ubiquitous in the verbal arts. There is little difficulty, to be sure, in recognizing the primary rhetorical dimensions in the *Junius Letters*, Dr. Johnson's *Taxation No Tyranny*, Paine's *Rights of Man*, Swift's *Allies*. Rhetorical criticism as we define it can illumine them in their natural contexts. On the other hand, though not quite so readily, one may see significant rhetorical dimensions in Dr. Johnson's *Rambler* or *Rasselas*, in Swift's *Drapier's Letters* or *Modest Proposal* or *Gulliver*, even in Marvel's *Coy Mistress* or Goldsmith's *Deserted Village*, in Lewis' *Babbitt* or Hemingway's *For Whom the Bell Tolls*.

Some possibilities for the rhetorical in the criticism of literature I have explored briefly in the Iowa booklet of 1965, mentioned earlier, and in the last page or two of an article of 1966 called "Edmund Burke: The New Images."[29] My view in those essays is related to the view of Edward Corbett in the introduction to his recent anthology, *Rhetorical Analysis of Literary Works*. Corbett, like Wayne Booth in *The Rhetoric of Fiction*, considers the rhetorical as the basis of an author's engagement with his reader, of those elements or strategies in the work through which the reader (or in drama the spectator) is brought to accept the world which the author has created. Rhetorical criticism, therefore, says Corbett,

> is that mode of internal criticism which considers the interactions between the work, the author, and the audience. As such it is interested in the *product*, the *process*, and the *effect* of linguistic activity, whether of the imaginative kind or the utilitarian kind. When rhetorical criticism is applied to imaginative literature, it regards the work not so much as an object of contemplation but as an artistically structured instrument for communication. It is more interested in a literary work for what it *does* than for what it is.[30]

---

[29] Donald C. Bryant, "Edmund Burke: The New Images," *Quarterly Journal of Speech*, LII (1966), 329–36.

[30] Edward P. J. Corbett, *Rhetorical Analysis of Literary Works* (New York: Oxford University Press, 1969), xxii.

Of course, I would not limit the rhetorical dimensions of criticism, even of literary works, to factors within the fictional world only. No matter what the writer's "intent," novels, plays, poems, personal essays do alter perception and behavior in what Northrop Frye calls the world of social action and event[31] and hence function as public address. No doubt Sir Herbert Read is right that in art it is not the message but the mode of conveyance which matters.[32] Rhetoricians know, however, that the mode of conveyance provides much of the message. They did not need McLuhan to tell them that; and they know that *Oliver Twist*, however intended, could touch the available responses of the social conscience of England as vividly as the lectures and sermons of Charles Kingsley.

Here I shall leave my current view of the chief features of that mode of criticism which is grounded in a rationale of the informative and suasory in discourse. Subsequently I intend to offer critical studies of some primarily rhetorical artifacts, both oral and written. It may be that those studies will exemplify principles I have been treating. If so, I shall be fortunate, for as a notable poet-critic is said to have replied to one who sensed disparity between his critical doctrine and his poetic practice, "A man may think what he pleases, but he must write what he can."

[31] Northrop Frye, *The Anatomy of Criticism* (Princeton: Princeton University Press, 1957), 243.
[32] Sir Herbert Read, *Art and Society* (3rd ed.; London: Heinemann, 1956), 204.

III

The Rhetorical Art of Edmund Burke:
Wilkes and the Middlesex Election, 1769

The rhetorical art of Edmund Burke is yet to be described comprehensively or assayed definitively. Perhaps it cannot be, yet, for Burke is still a figure of active controversy; and the atmosphere of controversy is not ideal for judicious criticism and rational appraisal of an art so organically a part of the medium of controversy as the rhetorical is.[1] No doubt the opportunity offered herein should impel me to the attempt, but I shall modestly decline. Instead, I shall explore some of the essential considerations involved in such a comprehensive description and assessment.

Burke was born in Dublin in 1729, the year of Jonathan Swift's *A Modest Proposal*, that devastating attack on British oppression of Ireland. His father was a Protestant lawyer; his mother, a Roman Catholic from the south. Edmund was

---

[1] I do not mean to imply that criticism of Burke is scarce or meager among biographers, historians of ideas, or critics of literature and politics. Most such criticism, however, is and has been focused and limited, naturally enough, by the interests and biases of the critic. Burke, for example, was one of the prime subjects for the "literary criticism of oratory" in Herbert A. Wichelns, "The Literary Criticism of Oratory," in Alexander M. Drummond (ed.), *Studies in Rhetoric and Public Speaking in Honor of James Albert Winans* (New York: Century Co., 1925). It is the "rhetorical" criticism of Burke which has had the least thorough attention. W. E. H. Lecky in his *A History of England in the Eighteenth Century* (8 vols.; London, 1878–1890; New York: Appleton, 1891)

reared a Protestant; he had his preparatory education at a Quaker school in the country and his advanced education at the Anglican Trinity College, Dublin. At Trinity he organized and conducted a lively undergraduate literary and debating society and, at the age of nineteen, wrote *The Reformer*, a weekly periodical in the traditon of *The Spectator*, modestly intended to improve the taste of Dublin theatergoers and the quality of their fare!

Burke's subsequent achievements are known variously to students of literature and politics today. Some know him as the author of the theoretic-aesthetic treatise on the *Origin of our Ideas of the Sublime and Beautiful* (1757). Others, especially students of public address and of American colonial history, know his speech-pamphlets, *American Taxation* (1774) and *Conciliation with America* (1775), and perhaps his *Letter to the Sheriffs of Bristol on the Affairs of America* (1777) which I shall later discuss at some length. Some people will pigeonhole him, perhaps, as the father of conservatism; others, as a Wilsonian liberal. Those who follow the history of literary institutions may remember that Edmund Burke, with Oliver Goldsmith the playwright-poet-novelist-essayist and the painter-critic Sir Joshua Reynolds, was one of the original members of Dr. Samuel Johnson's famous club, and was, after Johnson, its primary conversationalist.[2]

Whichever Burke you prefer is a real Burke; and there are perhaps others just as real, for the last quarter-century has seen a remarkable acceleration and proliferation of Burke

---

and Viscount John Morley in his biography, *Burke*, in the English Men of Letters Series (London: Macmillan, 1882) have come the nearest to treating Burke as *rhetor*. Of recent brief characterizations I find most satisfactory that by W. J. Bate in his introduction to *Edmund Burke: Selected Works* (New York: Modern Library, 1960).

[2] See Donald C. Bryant, "Edmund Burke's Conversation," in *Studies in Speech and Drama in Honor of Alexander M. Drummond* (Ithaca: Cornell University Press, 1944), 354–68.

studies—editions, biographies, anthologies, debunkings, analyses, reconstructions, idolatries, and what not.[3] From them has come a new Burke every year or so. From the thorough scholarship of the investigators of the newly available Burke papers and the editors of his correspondence comes an enlarged, a deepened, a freshly illumined, but still generally familiar Burke.[4] From the microcosmic history of Sir Lewis Namier and his students and competitors comes the deflated Burke of the "fertile, disordered, and malignant imagination,"[5] who imposed a false conception of politics and of George III upon superior men in his own time who should have known better, and upon the "Whig historians" of a subsequent century and a quarter. From the American neo-conservatives such as Russell Kirk[6] and company comes the reconstituted idol of the Right—the intellectual conservative, the anti-Jacobin anti-Democrat turned anti-Communist, who had been sadly misunderstood by the Leckys, the Morleys, the Wilsons, and other nineteenth-century liberals. And from neo-Thomists and the new Christian Humanists comes the long-undiscovered apostle of natural law, the champion who can put down not only the Tom Paines and the atheistic egalitarians, but now the Bolshevist anti-Christ whom all

---

[3] I surveyed this literature extensively through 1962 in a review essay, "Edmund Burke: A Generation of Scholarship and Discovery," *Journal of British Studies*, II (November, 1962), 91-114. Output has hardly slackened since.

[4] The new *Correspondence of Edmund Burke* (Cambridge, Eng.: Cambridge University Press; and Chicago: University of Chicago Press, 1958 ——), under the general editorship of Thomas W. Copeland, is complete except for Volume X, the general index. Carl Cone's *Burke and the Nature of Politics* (2 vols; Lexington, Ky.: University of Kentucky Press, 1957, 1964) is the first extended biographical study to use the papers liberally.

[5] L. B. Namier, "Monarchy and the Party System," *Personalities and Powers* (London and New York: Macmillan, 1955), 21.

[6] See, for example, Russell Kirk, *The Conservative Mind* (Chicago: Regnery, 1953), Ch. II, "Burke and the Politics of Prescription"; and Kirk's *Edmund Burke: A Genius Reconsidered* (New Rochelle, N.Y.: Arlington House, 1967).

freedom-loving Americans abhor.[7] Surrounding, suffusing, and incarnating them all, however, is Burke the rhetor, the accomplished thinker-writer-speaker functioning in the day-to-day and year-to-year controversies of his time—and by extension, of subsequent times even to our own.

Characterizations of Burke the writer-speaker are endemic in commentaries on eighteenth-century British history and literature. It could not be otherwise, and it is just as inevitable that they should range from the idolatrous through the judicious to the belittling and the polemic. In the headnote to Burke in a recent anthology I have distilled what I take to be friendly but not idolatrous judgments of the distinguishing features of Burke's public rhetorical output:

> The largeness of view which it encompassed; the broad, deep knowledge which it exhibited; the fullness with which it developed particular problems in detail and in historical perspective [and context]; the clarity [and vividness] with which it related those problems to general principles of morality and human nature; and the happy fusion of emotion and reasoning which is the characteristic of eloquence and good literature. His imagination gives form and energy to the politics and the morality; his metaphoric expression does not merely decorate the thought, it incarnates the thought, it creates the idea. In his . . . speaking and writing Burke brought literature and politics into a union which had not been so close or so equal since Cicero.
>
> [But] these very qualities in Burke have caused critics in his own time and since to laud the writer and deplore the speaker, to compare him unfavorably with Fox, for example, as tedious and ineffective, as . . . [the] extravagant orator rather than . . . [the] parliamentary debater, as too long, lush, and literary.[8]

Each element in the foregoing could be documented from

---

[7] The leading proponent of this view and founder of the scholarly journal *Studies in Burke and His Time*, is Peter J. Stanlis. See his *Edmund Burke and the Natural Law* (Ann Arbor: University of Michigan Press, 1958).

[8] Donald C. Bryant *et al.* (eds.), *An Historical Anthology of Select British Speeches* (New York: Ronald Press, 1967), 213.

witnesses from Burke's time to ours; but we should remind ourselves again of the political commonplace that it is difficult to think completely ill of incompetence in a person who supports one's favorite position, or to appreciate properly the excellence of one's most formidable opponents.

In this and a subsequent essay I propose to examine critically Burke's rhetorical art in two quite different contexts and manifestations: first, in the staple of parliamentary activity, extemporaneous debate; and second in his final major publication on American affairs. The first is the situation in which Burke traditionally is said not to have excelled, in fact not even to have been good. It is the situation in which he is almost always contrasted with Charles James Fox, to Burke's disadvantage. The second is a situation in which Burke has been praised often, perhaps even beyond any man's deserts. Burke as debater, though freely disparaged by commentators, has seldom been carefully examined. Critics seem to have taken the word of Oliver Goldsmith[9] and a few others and let it go at that. One reason, of course, is that whereas we are plentifully supplied with full, authentic texts of Burke's major works, most of his speaking in the House, like everyone else's, is very poorly reported. That is a difficulty which we are now able in part to overcome as we examine early Burke on the floor of the Commons.

When Burke entered the House of Commons in January of 1766, after six months as secretary and assistant to the Marquess of Rockingham, the new first minister, he had reached

---

[9] *Retaliation*, ll. 29–42, where Goldsmith seems to launch what still appears to survive as the "dinner bell" characterization of Burke's parliamentary speaking. See Donald C. Bryant, "The Contemporary Reception of Edmund Burke's Speaking," in *Studies in Honor of Frederick W. Shipley*, by His Colleagues (St. Louis: Washington University Studies, 1942), 245–64; reprinted, revised and enlarged, in Raymond F. Howes (ed.), *Historical Studies of Rhetoric and Rhetoricians* (Ithaca: Cornell University Press, 1961), 271–93.

the mature age of thirty-seven (not a precocious but still malleable nineteen like Charles James Fox when he made his parliamentary debut). Burke's cast of mind, his habits of thought and language, his fundamental store of general knowledge, and his industry in reading and investigation may be presumed to have been already basically established. Besides his reading in London for the law, for which he never qualified, and besides his publication of the *Sublime and Beautiful* and his satire on Bolingbroke, Burke had served in political Dublin under William Gerard Hamilton, secretary to the Lord-Lieutenant, had contributed largely to a history of European colonies in America, and had founded and written for Dodsley the *Annual Register*, a volume in current history for which Burke observed and recorded the whole breadth of British and European politics. He might be expected to develop in certain ways as he became domesticated to the new environment and the new medium and as he reconciled his talents and his resources to the special circumstances of the House of Commons. Indeed the testimony of his letters is explicit on the point.

Very quickly Burke made himself a man of importance in his party and in Parliament, but he was certainly not—like Charles Fox and the younger Pitt—a "child of the House,"[10] as he later called Charles Townshend: one nurtured, licked into shape, so to speak, by the Commons. Politics and Parliament did not so much form Burke the thinker-speaker-writer in public affairs as offer him a special environment wherein he could function and develop rhetorically in the fashion for which he was fitted.

Only three days after the opening of his first session, Burke screwed up his nerve to make his maiden speech, the custom-

[10] Edmund Burke, *Speech on American Taxation, The Works of the Right Honorable Edmund Burke* (12 vols.; Boston: Little, Brown, 1894), II, 68.

ary trauma of which he immediately described to Charles O'Hara, his political father in Ireland: "I know not what struck me, but I took a sudden resolution to say something. . . . I did say something; what it was I know not upon my honour; I felt like a man drunk. . . . All I hoped was to plunge in, & get off the first horrors; I had no hopes of making a figure. I find my Voice not strong enough to fill the house; but I shall endeavour to raise it as high as it will bear."[11]

Almost immediately thereafter Burke was performing in debate with the energy, the apparent confidence, and sometimes the recklessness of the seasoned soldier and parliamentary Cossack, the ally of Pitt, Colonel Isaac Barré. He was performing also with a knowledge of the affairs of empire, of commerce, and of constitutional history which was extraordinary in any member, much less a so-called "young" member. In March, Lord Charlemont, Burke's Irish friend and admirer, wrote Henry Flood of Burke's "unparalleled success," and remarked, "His character daily rises, and Barré is totally eclipsed by him; his praise is universal, and even the Opposition, who own his superior talents, can find nothing to say against him, but that he is an impudent fellow."[12]

For Burke's earliest speeches we have practically no reliable texts, though it has been possible to reconstruct from partially burnt notes among his papers and from an outside source or two an approximation of his principal speech on the repeal of the Stamp Act.[13] On the other hand, as everybody knows, we do have abundant and almost completely laudatory witnesses to his almost immediate distinction in speaking. The testimony of most of those witnesses I brought to focus

---

[11] Copeland (ed.) *Correspondence*, I, 232–33.
[12] *Ibid.*, 243 *n.* 3.
[13] Thomas H. D. Mahoney, "Edmund Burke and the American Revolution: The Repeal of the Stamp Act," in Peter J. Stanlis *et al.* (eds.), *Edmund Burke: The Enlightenment and the Modern World* (Detroit: University of Detroit Press, 1967), 8–12.

some time ago in an article entitled "The Contemporary Reception of Burke's Speaking."[14]

By 1768, when from the shorthand transcripts of Sir Henry Cavendish we first have something approaching verbatim texts of debates in the House of Commons—that is, by the time Charles Fox first took his seat in the House (on the side of government), and when the "Great Commoner" had gone to the House of Lords as Earl of Chatham—Burke had come very close to being the leading speaker in the Commons and, except for Chatham's occasional appearances, in all of Parliament. He was soon to publish his first important political pieces: *On the Present State of the Nation* (1769), an impressive fiscal and political reply to the Grenvillite William Knox; and *Thoughts on the Cause of the Present Discontents* (1770), his celebrated manifesto of the Rockingham party. So far, however, his reputation was as speaker and man of business in the House of Commons, not yet as formidable controversial writer too. The historian Dame Lucy S. Sutherland, longtime principal of Lady Margaret Hall, Oxford, and one of the editors of the new *Correspondence*, writes of this period:

> His outstanding asset to his party, in addition to his loyalty and enthusiasm, was without question the possession of those qualities to which the eighteenth-century House of Commons and the political public were so susceptible, the gift of oratory and the power of debate. Though his own references to his successes are few and modest, his friends were ecstatic in their reports of his power to move his hearers, to range over the most diverse problems, and to clarify complex issues. Habitually speaking late in debates in the House (it was not for him at this time to open debates for his party [that was William Dowdeswell's function]), he was capable both of keeping the House "in continuous laughter" with his humour and sarcasm, and of making important issues appear grave and momentous.... He was also an indefatigable and telling debater, though here cer-

---

[14] Note 9 above.

tain faults of judgment and temperament sometimes marred his usefulness.[15]

If in these early years Burke exhibited characteristics in debate which his critics could turn to his discredit, he himself was well aware of the characteristics and he had no intention of changing them. He confessed to his old school friend Richard Shackleton in the spring of 1770: "It is but too well known, that I debate with great Vehemence and asperity and with very little management either of the opinions or persons of many of my adversaries. They deserve not much Quarter, and I give and receive but very little"[16]

Almost as soon as he began to be heard often in the House, those who wished to deprecate or belittle his manner of speaking and his influence complained that he refused to let ordinary subjects remain ordinary, to speak in commonplace language, familiar images, and comfortable platitudes to the ordinary intellect and confined interests of the average country member. After a month or so of his first session he wrote to O'Hara: "Those who don't wish me well, say I am abstracted and subtile; perhaps it is true; I myself don't know it; but think, if I had not been known to be the Author of a Book somewhat metaphysical [the *Sublime and Beautiful*], the objections against my mode of Argument would be of another nature, and possibly more just. However until I know better, I intend to follow my own way."[17] He followed his own way, and a special way it was—a way of notable excellences, but also of conspicuous hazards. In Cavendish's reports and in Burke's notes and drafts preserved in the Fitzwilliam Papers, the principal characteristics of that way are already well established and are only to become heightened with use and changing circumstances as the writer-speaker advances in

[15] Copeland (ed.), *Correspondence*, II, xii.
[16] *Ibid.*, 130.
[17] *Ibid.*, I, 241.

consequence and comes to grips with more and more serious problems and more and more capable opponents.

To study Burke's rhetorical art in debate in these early years, prior to his major involvement in American affairs, we may turn profitably to the debates recorded by that assiduous shorthand artist and member of Parliament, Henry Cavendish,[18] rather than to Burke's famous set pieces published by him for the record and for controversy outside Parliament. These are resources with which general students of the period are least likely to be familiar, and through Cavendish's so-called "Parliamentary Diary" we may get around the inadequate reporting in the public press. The speaking of Burke which I have chosen to investigate is that constituting part of the protracted and frustrating debates over John Wilkes and the Middlesex election of late 1768 and early 1769.

It would be interesting to review in detail the long sequence of bitter conflicts centering in that popular demagogue (or as some might say, radical agitator), from the battle over No. 45 of *The North Briton* in 1763 to the prosecution of the printers in 1771. Those conflicts became intense, in Parliament and out, in 1763 when Wilkes was arrested on a general warrant for seditious libel on the King in No. 45 of his paper *The North Briton.* He went into voluntary exile in Paris to avoid prosecution. The next year he was expelled from the House of Commons and was declared outlaw for writing *The North Briton* and publishing an obscene *Essay on Woman.* Thus did Wilkes generate controversy at least as late as his provocative in-

---

[18] Cavendish, who sat in the House of Commons from 1768 to 1774, had learned shorthand apparently with the intention of recording and publishing as full as possible a text of the debates. Transcriptions of his notes (some still in shorthand) are preserved in Egerton MSS 215–262 and 3711 in the British Museum as the Cavendish Parliamentary Diary. Though his record suffers from gaps and omissions and is obviously not altogether verbatim, it is a better report than others of the debates of the time. The reports from 1768 into 1771 were edited and published by John Wright as *Sir Henry Cavendish's Debates of the House of Commons . . .* (2 vols.; London: Longman, 1841–43).

volvement in the House of Commons' prosecution of the London printers in 1771. Suffice it now to recall that Wilkes returned from his voluntary exile in Paris in 1768, still under the 1764 decree of outlawry. He was received enthusiastically by the corporation and populace of London, but failed to gain a seat in Commons. He immediately stood for the county of Middlesex, was elected, surrendered to his outlawry, and went to prison. His outlawry was soon reversed, and on May 10 the crowds that gathered in St. George's Fields to escort Wilkes from prison to Parliament were fired on by troops authorized by the secretaries of state and war to assist the civil magistrates. At least one civilian was killed, but the offending soldier was exonerated and the troops were officially thanked by the secretary. Wilkes obtained a copy of the letter from Lord Weymouth, the secretary of state, authorizing necessary precautions against riots; prefaced it with a note accusing the secretary of preplanned massacre; and had it printed in the *St. James Chronicle.* The House of Lords declared Wilkes guilty of insolent, scandalous, and seditious libel against one of its members, and asked the Commons' concurrence. After much debate government prevailed. Wilkes was denied his request for a hearing, the preface was declared libelous, and Wilkes was expelled. He was reelected by large majorities three times, was expelled each time, and finally his last opponent, Colonel Luttrell, was declared elected.

The conflict centering on Wilkes enabled a chafing opposition, frustrated in its ambition to unseat the ministry of Grafton and North, to exploit such basic and ever-attractive issues as freedom of the press, immunity of members of Parliament from civil arrest, use of military force in civil disturbances (much like our popular issue of "police brutality"), the rights of electors freely to choose their representatives, constitutional separation of powers, and abuse of the laws of libel to suppress dissidence in Parliament.

The debate over the condemnation, expulsion, and disqualification of Wilkes by the House of Commons displayed strong feeling and little inhibition on both sides. Of the especially provocative factors at work, two were foremost. First, the king and the ministry were determined to save face by quieting Wilkes or getting rid of him. Secondly, Wilkes was equally determined to be as objectionable as necessary in order not to be pardoned or ignored.

Joined with these factors was the notorious private character of Wilkes, which had been a source of public amusement at least since the issue of the purloined and indecent *Essay on Woman* of 1763.[19] All speakers made a point of deploring Wilkes's private character, those against the prosecution using their moral disapproval as prelude to finding in Wilkes the incarnation of popular resistance to autocratic government.

At the same time that passions ran high, ingenuity of argument soon ran out—rhetorical invention dried up though conflict continued. As condemnation, denial of appeal, expulsion, and more expulsion dragged on, there was soon little new in substance to say to justify or oppose the redundant actions. There was only new "foul" to be called, new "tyranny" to be decried, new "personalities" to be hurled, and old lines of argument to be revived, redecorated, and if possible recharged.

During the debates Burke's attendance in his place on the

---

[19] During the *North Briton* trouble, Wilkes, at a private press in his own house, had printed a few copies of a parody of Pope's *Essay on Man* called *An Essay on Woman*, and a parody of the *Veni Creator*, both of which could be thought indecent and even blasphemous. Wilkes, who probably had a hand in writing them, intended them for circulation among the club of profligate bloods with whom he associated. He never published the pieces, but during the general warrant operation, proofs were stolen from his premises and were exhibited to the House of Lords (including, of course, the bishops) with scandalized delight by the Earl of Sandwich, one of the notorious libertines of the time and a member of Wilkes's club.

opposition side of the House was regular and ernest. He spoke often—one significant speech near the end of debate on each motion—but not remarkably long. Burke never opened a debate until he offered the first original motion of his career on March 8, when he attempted to reopen consideration of military intervention in the affair of St. George's Fields. On the matter of Wilkes, his responses and his attacks were ready, relevant, and usually imaginative. For example, following a vehement speech by Lord North charging Wilkes with libel on Lord Weymouth, Burke rejoined thus: "I am terrified, though not blasted, by the thunder of the noble lord; who hurls about his bolts, like the Thunderer of famous memory: but, Sir, judges ought not to be arrayed in thunder; the still silence of the Almighty ought to go before the thunder of this House."[20] Here is a partially jesting opening, which turns at once to the heart of the matter—the house as a judge of libel is resorting to very unjudicial polemic.

Burke certainly contributed his share to the repetition of arguments in support of Wilkes; after all, to retain self-respect and status for the Opposition he had to keep on debating. And he generated his share of the vehemence and passion. In addition, however, he often infused fresh impetus into the stalled argument and into the attack on ministers. Furthermore, he insistently enlarged the context of the particular incident or the particular issue through recourse to history and analogy. And he sought a moral dimension for the argument by rising out of the immediate circumstance to political, social, and philosophical generalization.

Of Burke's many contributions to the protracted controversy, the most interesting and still characteristic is probably that he made toward the end of the debate on the secretary at war's motion of February 3, 1769, for the initial expulsion

---

[20] Wright (ed.), *Cavendish Debates,* I, 109.

after the condemnation for libel.[21] On that speech I shall concentrate our examination.

Wilkes, the Opposition had argued, was being expelled from the Commons for an accumulation of offenses, each satisfying one or other supporter of the Administration but no one offense seeming criminal to the majority as a whole. Burke refurbished the argument in a couple of fresh analogies after opening with a witty gambit at the expense of the principal speakers for the Government: "They who were lawyers at the beginning of the week are now, at the end of the debate, become men of wit,—deciding a great national concern upon motives of private resentment, and doing very bad actions in a good-humoured manner." Then to complete the enthymeme on political morality: "Sir, men with good-humoured faces have signed papers that have made nations tremble." Barrington and Weymouth, the secretaries of state and war, had "signed papers" before and after the recent unhappiness in St. George's Fields, which Burke and his friends thought should make England tremble for its civil government.

Next, with a metaphor and a "good-humoured" analogy, Burke demolished the legality of the expulsion: "Accumulative crimes are things unknown to the courts below [Parliament, of course is the highest court]: that is not their arithmetic; in those courts, two bad things will not make one capital offense. This is serving up like cooks: some will eat of one dish, some of another; so there will not be a fragment left." The bare comparison, however, which would have contented a Dowdeswell, a Grenville, or a Fox—if perchance their imaginations had leapt that far—and might even have satisfied a Colonel Barré, would not serve to liven the issue and amuse the House with the vividness that Burke thought appropriate. Nor would it with enough sharp ridicule expose the

---

[21] *Ibid.*, 179–82.

disunity and personal enmities within the Government's voting phalanx. Besides, when Burke once got started on a figure —as the notes and drafts among his manuscript papers bear witness again and again—the figure was likely to take command of his imagination and furnish for him the structure of a passage if not the substance of an argument.[22] So Burke on this occasion elaborated the metaphor of the cook, to discredit one after another of the Government's speakers. Their argument had often gone back to the so-called scandal six years before, of Wilkes's *Essay on Woman;* of this, Burke said:

> Some will like the strong, solid roast beef of the blasphemous libel. One honourable member could not bear to see Christianity abused, because it was part of the common law of England—not because it was a part of common reason: this is solid, substantial, roast beef reasoning. I see strong party zeal in what you are doing; but I proceed to show how the gentlemen on the other side of the House have acted upon this occasion. These gentlemen appear to pay little regard to the blasphemy; still there is something in the cookery that offends them. The libel upon the Crown, that does not much trouble them—they have given up the libel upon the Crown; but the libel upon the minister [Lord Weymouth, one of themselves], that many gentlemen, heterogeneous in their composition, have been perfectly in earnest in their reprobation of.

After thus draining the juices from the analogy of cookery, Burke summarized the confusion in a paradox and brought all together in a theatrical parody and topical image:

> Thus it is hoped that what hits them in their several capacities will produce an unanimity, upon the principles of discord. The late hour of the night—the candles [for lighting old St. Stephens Chapel where Commons met]—all put me in mind of the representation of the last act of a tragi-

---

[22] Recall the Dauphiness on the balcony at Versailles in the *Reflections on the Revolution in France,* or the "Triple Keep of Windsor" in *A Letter to a Noble Lord,* in *Works,* III, 331–32, and V, 210.

comedy, performed by his Majesty's servants, by desire of several persons of distinction, for the benefit of Mr. Wilkes and at the expense of the constitution. But [he continued] these masters of political drama have not done everything cleverly on this occasion: no man can see from one part of the plot to the other; every act seems to lead to different results.

Satisfied now, apparently, with the effects of his parody, Burke anticipated defensive response to his humor from the other side. Such a response had come as recently as a day or two earlier from Richard Rigby, the principal spokesman of the Duke of Bedford and one of the reliable debaters from Administration. Said Burke: "To some this may seem to be ridiculous, and the honourable gentleman will call it declamation; but, nevertheless, I shall make it appear to be sound argument."

And so he did. He developed a firmly reasoned, legal, historical argument. And he emphasized his shift from metaphor to argument by flaunting the technical language of logic and the shape of rhetorical partition:

> When you come to this question of discretion, it will require to be considered with regard to all its *circumstances*, with regard to all its *adjuncts*, with regard to any *consequences* that are likely to flow from it. All these are *necessary* considerations: it is a question of justice, of fundamental justice; it is a question of prudence; it is a question of the dignity of this House; it is a question of the approbation of the public; which approbation, if it does not follow your acts, those acts, I will venture to say, will have no useful consequences. [Italics mine.]

Then, closing the passage in his characteristic ascent to general political morality, he drew his warning into a kind of *sententia*: "They who do injustice in order to get rid of an inconvenience, will give rise to an injustice which will react upon themselves." And two or three minutes later, after he had redeveloped Opposition's much belabored argument that expulsion of Wilkes on vengeful grounds could lead to the expulsion of any member objectionable to the majority, Burke raised the argument to another *sententia:* "One act of oppression generally leads to another: violence once begun will probably lead on to violence; it will not end with the beginning of it."

In the heat of such a debate, when no new substantive arguments could be advanced, but only familiar ones reiterated, refurbished, and recharged, bare reasoning sustained for a considerable length of time could hardly have been expected of Burke and would not have been what was needed. As the speech developed, he did not revive the figure and the fiction of his opening, the satiric analogy of cookery; but at one point, he echoed the analogy in a brief dramatization of the diverse statements actually made by the enemies of Wilkes:

> When this business first came before you, one gentleman said, he meant Mr. Wilkes's petition to be the ground of expulsion; another told us, he intended the records should be that ground; another, the message from the House of Lords. "I come into this resolution," says a fourth, "because of his censure upon the conduct of a great magistrate." Then comes the letter of the secretary of state. "Why! in times of danger," says a fifth, "I am afraid of doing any thing that will shake the government." Sir, if those gentlemen had spoken the truth, and told you what they really meant to found the motion of expulsion upon, it would not have been attended with success.

The language of imagery, some of it pretty strong, continued to pervade the speech. By the expulsion, Wilkes would be "blotched all over," would be "made leprous all over." The proposed action would "put the last hand to the liberty of the press. If you punish the excess it will cease to be a liberty at all." "The House of Commons, Sir, is not an assembly of inquisitors, but an assembly of gentlemen, or they do not represent those who sent them thither." "The ministry piece out the lion's skin with the fox's tail; they pour out all the vials of court wrath" upon Wilkes (not a very novel figure!) "and, by doing so, endeavor to cover the shame and nakedness of their own proposition."

Biblical phrasing and biblical echoes often pervaded Burke's language and substance, as any close student of the *Speech on Conciliation* knows well. In the present speech, warning the majority that it was setting a precedent which, given a slight change of circumstances, might be used against any of its members, he asked, "Is every gentleman in this House so pure in heart, so sure in conversation, that there may not be one word that a treacherous friend may steal from him." (Much of the evidence against Wilkes as author of the *Essay on Woman* had been stolen from his private rooms.) "Though the minister may now be sheltered in a warm majority," he went on, "a majority is but a fair flower; it flourishes in the morning, and in the evening it is as grass and |is| cast into the minority; growing up in these gardens, it is blasted before night." Here, of course, both the familiarity of the biblical echo and the wit of the parody would serve to enliven interest—and to generate amusement.

It seems as if Burke was artistically comfortable only when his reasonings could be generalized into *sententiae* or resolved into metaphor. For example, in this speech, while he is arguing the primacy of law over vengeance, syllogism blends quickly into domestic metaphor; it is then reinforced by balanced, reversible aphorism; and finally it turns again to metaphor and to god- and devil-terms. Thus:

> The question is, whether you shall proceed against the crime, or the man. If you punish the crime, the law is sufficient for you: the crime and the law reside with one another. It has been said by somebody, find me a crime and I will find you a man; but the administration say, find me

a man and we will find a crime. The destruction of the man is the object. A man is in complete armour, who is covered by the law; there is a little opening in the armour where justice may enter. Is parliament the fit instrument of such violence?

To conclude his modest effort at "nondeclamation," Burke once more defied his belittling critics in a passionate reinforcement of the main issue:

Here, Sir, I make my stand. Let us save the Parliament: let us be considered as the great advisers of the Crown. If Mr. Wilkes is a triumphant man, cease to persecute him and he dies in a moment; disappoint him. Think how you have been troubled with much impertinence on his account. If you shut him out of the County of Middlesex, they will send you other popular members; all the counties of England will be libellers. The county of Middlesex says, "we will have our member;" you say, "shut him out;" we say, "let him come in." Such a scene of libelling is opening upon us as I dread to think of. Would to God I had colors dipped in heaven to paint this mischief to you! Let me not be told, I again say, that I am declaiming, that this is declamation. I dread the consequences of this violent struggle between the two tides of power and popularity.

This is debating, a special kind of debating. It is aggressive refutation, where the reinforcement of evidence may be useful, but the logic of new argument is no longer possible or relevant; where humor, ridicule, and the other resources of imagination provide the ammunition with which to discredit the general position and the intention of the other side. For this kind of speaking Burke had special talent and, it seems, a special liking.

Perhaps it is an index of the impact—or the anticipated impact—of Burke's performance that he was answered by the most formidable speaker of administration, Lord North, who hit Burke where he had obviously expected to be hit, in his "declamation": "The honourable gentleman," said North, "is always terrifying himself where there is no danger"; and he threw at Burke the story of the shepherd boy who cried "wolf." Perhaps there is no other effective rejoinder to irony and metaphor than irony and metaphor.

The expulsion of Wilkes was carried, as Burke and everyone knew that it would be, by a large majority. Earl Temple, brother-in-law of Chatham, an enemy of Administration and a friend of Wilkes, wrote of the debate that every speaker for the majority "dwelt upon the crime he most detested," and disapproved of punishment for the rest. "The various flowers of their eloquence," he wrote in irony, "composed a most delightful nosegay." That is the kind of fragrant depreciation not infrequently leveled at Burke. But not this time. "Burke spoke admirably," wrote Temple.[23]

Burke's performance in the debates on the condemnation and expulsion of Wilkes—characteristic as it is of Burke at that time in his development—cannot stand, nor should it stand, as the norm of Burke in action on the floor of the House of Commons throughout his long career. That performance is the performance of early Burke, Burke of remarkable initial success and consequence, but not as yet Burke the eminent practitioner of various modes of rhetorical discourse. For characterizing Burke at this time, contemporaries could not compare him, as biographers and later critics have done, with Charles James Fox. Fox had taken his seat only the previous November and was not to establish his special reputation in debate for another five or six years. The obvious comparison matched Burke with Colonel Isaac Barré, the hard-hitting protégé of the Earl of Shelburne, spokesman in Commons of the Pitt-Shelburne positions and in debate a successor, in a sense, to Pitt (now Chatham in the House of Lords). Barré had

---

[23] Earl Temple to the Countess of Chatham, February 4, 1769, in William Stanhope Taylor and John Henry Pringle (eds.), *Correspondence of William Pitt, Earl of Chatham* (4 vols.; London: John Murray, 1839), III, 350.

sat in Parliament five years longer than Burke and had established an image of the ready, vigorous, uninhibited Opposition debater. Hence, as we have seen, when Burke's friends wished to assess his early reception in debate, they compared him with Barré.[24]

In certain respects the comparison is appropriate. We shall see later that Barré, like Burke, brought something fresh and interesting and formidable to debate in Commons. Barré, however, remained to the end the ready, reliable executor of rhetorical assignments, the debater in attack and defense, who spoke often and vehemently, but always briefly (as speeches went in those days). He was not the originator, initiator, formulator of policy or position, but the efficient, effective promoter on the floor. His part in the debate on Wilkes, for example, on the same side as Burke's, was strong and sure.

Burke also, as we have observed, had considerable talent and liking for the floor fight, and indeed the debate we have examined exhibits him in one of his perennial roles of witty and telling harassment. From the start, however, he was distinguished from Barré by the depth and breadth of his knowledge of the past and present in public affairs, and by his command of distinguished language. In December of 1767 that soldier of fortune and later controversial American general, Charles Lee, wrote to the Polish statesman Prince Czartoryski: "An Irishman, one Mr. Burke, is sprung up in the House of Commons, who has astonished every body with the power of his eloquence, his comprehensive knowledge in all our exterior and internal politics and commercial interests. He wants nothing but that sort of dignity annexed to rank and property in England, to make him the most considerable man in the Lower House."[25]

---

[24] Note 12, above.
[25] *The Lee Papers*, Vol. I, 1754–1776, *Collections of the New York Historical*

Burke continued to exhibit mastery of the substance of parliamentary controversy, in both ordinary, daily debate and more extended, preplanned speeches; and like Barré he sustained his uninhibited role in attack and defense on the floor of the House. That continued to be one of Burke's characteristic roles, as it did Barré's, but soon it was no longer his distinctive role, if it ever had been. As early as a month or so after the speech we have just examined, Burke changed his role from responder to initiator as he moved for a committee to inquire into the use of the military in the riots in St. George's Fields. His opening speech, of considerable scope and depth of detail, elicited from Attorney General DeGrey what came to be a stock resource for discrediting Burke's argument: "The honourable gentleman seems to think that I have mistaken his proposition. I do not mean to follow him in all the flights of his imagination; into those agreeable illusions of fancy which he indulges in, upon all occasions. I have taken down his words."[26] Two of Burke's colleagues in the debate, characteristically, came to the defense of his rhetorical mode. According to one, he had "abstained from all flights of fancy and imagination." Another declared, "Although my honourable friend possesses a larger stock of wit and humour than falls to the share of most men, no one could give less scope to his imagination, than he has done on this occasion. He has this day confined himself to giving us a proof of the goodness of his heart."[27]

Thus, one may say, Burke initiated what became his distinctive role in parliamentary speaking. It was a complex role, founded in a rhetorical art both refined and free. It was a role which is to be studied in his major oratorical undertakings, of

---

Society for the Year 1871 (New York: Printed for the Society, 1872), 61.
[26] Wright (ed.), *Cavendish Debates*, I, 320.
[27] *Ibid.*, 323, 325.

course, but also in the context of his day-to-day performance. When he is so studied, it will probably appear that the two kinds of performances together, in support and illumination of each other, characterize the distinctive Burkean rhetorical art.

The more intimately we examine Burke's speaking—the everyday debate as well as the more finished performances— the more cogent seems the remark once reported to Burke's literary friend Hannah More: "How closely that fellow reasons in metaphor!"[28] We will comprehend also the qualification attached by an anomymous parliamentary observer in 1774 to his praise of Burke's logical argument: "The speaker is capable . . . of the closest reasoning, as many of his speeches, much against his inclination testify."[29]

I have directed attention extensively to the foregoing illustration of the rhetorical art of Edmund Burke because it exemplifies the aspect with which students of the time are less likely to be acquainted and about which they are more likely to have picked up denigrating judgments. Even if those judgments be confirmed, at least they can rest upon the foundation of some small complement of direct evidence. I have attended to this material also because through observing the qualities of this kind of activity it may be possible to comprehend and perhaps account for the extended, prolific, and consequential part Burke played in the deliberations of the House of Commons, and of the public outside the House, for a period of thirty years.

---

[28] William Roberts, *Memoirs of the Life and Correspondence of Mrs. Hannah More* (4 vols.; London: Seeley and Burnside, 1834), III, 378.
[29] In one of a series of portraits of "Parliamentary Leaders" appearing in the summer of 1774. *Middlesex Journal,* No. 822 (July 4, 1774), p. 2, col. 1. Reprinted in *The Burke Newsletter,* V, No. 1 (Fall, 1963), 238–39.

IV

British Voices for America, 1765-1780

In roving freely and selectively through a body of public address which pervaded the atmosphere during one of the momentous crises in American history and in Anglo-American relations, I shall attempt to characterize and illustrate prime features of that discourse and of the men who presented it.

To set the tone of the exploration, we begin with a modest memory test and identification exercise. I shall quote without attribution passages from some of the louder voices for America heard during the progress of that notable transaction of which we are preparing to celebrate the bicentenary. In due course I shall attribute and identify the passages *in transit.* Initially one may have the satisfaction of testing his recollection.

The first is a passage many persons will recognize at once, though, perhaps, without being quite sure who spoke it.

> The proposition is peace. Not peace through the medium of war; not peace to be hunted through the labyrinth of intricate and endless negotiations; not peace to arise out of universal discord, fomented from principle . . . not peace to depend on the juridical determination of perplexing questions, or the precise marking the shadowy boundaries of a

complex government. It is simple peace, sought in its natural course and in its ordinary haunts. It is peace sought in the spirit of peace, and laid in principles purely pacific.[1]

The second, spoken ten years earlier than the first, will be familiar in substance, though perhaps not in this particular form:

> Believe me,—remember I this day told you so—that the same spirit which actuated that people at first will continue with them still. . . . I claim to know more of America than most of you, having seen and been conversant in that country. The people there are as truly loyal, I believe, as any subjects the king has; but a people jealous of their liberties, and who will vindicate them if they should be violated.

The next two will be hard to mistake, perhaps—the one spoken in the debate on the repeal of the Stamp Act, the other nearly twelve years later at the low point of American fortunes in the war:

> I rejoice that America has resisted.
>
>   *   *   *
>
> If I were an American, as I am an Englishman, while a foreign troop was landed in my country I never would lay down my arms—never! never! never!

That was the voice of an old and perpetual friend. Now comes a new recruit:

> I take this to be the question . . . whether America is to be governed by force, or management? I never could conceive that the Americans could be taxed without their consent.

[1] Were there, perhaps, echoes of this passage audible in the opening of President John F. Kennedy's address at the American University, June 10, 1963? "What kind of peace do we seek? Not a *Pax Americana* enforced on the world by American weapons of war. Not the peace of the grave or the security of the slave. I am talking about genuine peace, the kind of peace that makes life on earth worth living, the kind that enables men and nations to grow and to hope and to build a better life for their children—not merely peace for Americans, but peace for all men and women; not merely peace for our time, but peace for all time." John F. Kennedy, *The Burden and the Glory*, ed. by Allan Nevins (New York: Harper & Row, 1964), 53–54.

. . . There is not an American, but who must reject and resist the principle and right of our taxing them.

And finally, a voice, in a pamphlet, which may sound familiar to only a very few:

> Had we never deserted our old ground: Had we nourished and favoured *America*, with a view to commerce, instead of considering it as a country to be governed: had we, like a liberal and wise people, rejoiced to see a multitude of free states branched forth from ourselves, all enjoying independent legislatures similar to our own: . . . The Liberty of *America* might have preserved our Liberty; and under the direction of a patriot king or wise minister, proved the means of restoring our almost lost constitution.

Those are a few of the words of a few of the strong British voices for America, in Parliament and in print, before and during the armed conflict of the American Revolution.

Speaking of the friendly voices of two hundred years ago as we begin to get into the spirit of the bicentenary, the Spirit of '76, offers some obvious temptations. One is to freshen the portrait gallery of our reviving history with new likenesses of those enlightened characters who stood up to be counted as "Americans" in Britain during the approach of the American Revolution and the fighting of it. Their names, of course, are not conspicuous among the New Orleanses and the Baton Rouges on the one hand or the Jacksons and Monroes on the other here in Louisiana; but when one tours the old thirteen colonies from the Carolinas to New Hampshire, one finds them everywhere. Our forebears, naturally enough, seemed eager to pay their respects and to show their gratitude to their British sympathizers, and of course to enhance their own status, by naming their towns—or renaming them—for their "kinsmen" across the Atlantic. And, without being statistically finicky, I will observe that they were especially attracted to the names of those whose voices were heard loudly and persistently before and during the War of Independence. William Pitt, Earl of Chatham, is scattered liberally from state to state: Pittsburgh, Pennsylvania; Pittsfield, Massachusetts; Pittsylvania County, Virginia; Chatham, New York; and Chatham, Massachusetts, for example. Pitt's special parliamentary lieutenant Barré shows up in Vermont, Massachusetts, and tandem with the celebrated agitator in Wilkes-Barre, Pennsylvania. Rockingham is preserved in North Carolina, New Hampshire, and Virginia; but alas for my hypothesis! Burke seems not to have caught on, and I doubt that Fox Meadow was named after Charles James.

But enough of conjuring with nostalgic names. The important matter for us now, and a matter well known to our colonial ancestors, is that from the other side of the Atlantic the American problem and war were aspects of a national uneasiness over conditions at home as well as conditions over here. In important ways they were certainly as much political-social struggles among Englishmen at home as they were contentions and battles between Englishmen on the one side of the Atlantic and their dissident colonists on the other. The sharp, black-and-white simplifications and the accompanying personifications set up by Patrick Henry, and by Jefferson in the Declaration of Independence, are characteristic agitational strategies which seem usually to be necessary for focusing popular causes. But we know, and so did our ancestors, though they could not always admit it, that all American colonials were not Sam Adamses, Patrick Henrys, or Tom Paines, and that all Englishmen at home were not George III's, Lord Norths, Grenvilles, or Sam Johnsons. We know that professed devotion to "Liberty" on the one hand or hankering after "Tyranny" on the other was not the exclusive preoccupation of either side of the ocean in the political struggle.

I am not going to venture a "new" interpretation of the

causes and conduct of the War of Independence—or as it was generally called in England, the American War. I have none to offer, and of course others will be better equipped than I to reinterpret that history. My theme herein is the rhetorical factor in an important—perhaps a decisive—political-social-economic-ideological conflict in our past. By *rhetorical factor* I mean, of course, the argumentative and agitational speaking and writing. I shall focus attention chiefly upon the parliamentary speaking of a few of the principal persons who, from various positions and with sundry diverse and divergent motives, found common ground in American policy for their opposition to George III's government and his ministers.

The voices for America came from a wide spectrum of political, social, ideological contexts. Some of them were mutually at odds, except for their opposition to taxing the colonists and to using force to hold the colonies in due subordination to the Mother Country. The London radicals—the intractible Wilkesites—were one group. They advocated annual rather than septennial elections, reapportionment of the seats in the House of Commons, broadening the franchise even to universal manhood suffrage, binding members of Parliament by the instructions of their constituents, and the like. These supporters of the Americans had little ideologically or practically in common with the phalanx of Old Whig aristocracy and its middle-class adherents—the rightful heirs, in their view, of the Revolution Settlement of 1688—for whom Edmund Burke was the master spokesman. Both of these chiefly antagonistic groups, however, saw themselves as defenders of liberty, of the people, of the sacred rights of Englishmen. The one saw the "people" in the vast bulk of humanity exemplified in the workingmen of London, the farm laborers, the weavers of the Midlands. To the other, though the "people" may have been much the same, they were wards of the benevolent, enlightened nobility and gentry and the substantial merchants, those leisured and propertied men with a major stake in public office and government, and the time and resources to bear the burden of them. Both groups thought themselves disadvantaged, oppressed (or at least threatened) by men and measures and the social-political climate of the time; and each could look distantly across the Atlantic and with differing filters in their vision could see the freedom-loving Englishmen in the colonies as their brothers (or children) and their surrogates.

From their view of the Americans the several groups could generate and fashion common arguments and appeals to support their attacks on government and the system, and at the same time they could derive strength for their divergent primary interests—let us say, for example, commercial prosperity joined with so-called "popular" government; or the enlargement of empire at the expense of France; or freedom and political equality for Protestant Dissenters.

The principal and most accomplished speakers and writers in the cause of America tended to cluster, in one degree or another of dependency or alliance, either around William Pitt, Earl of Chatham, "The Great Commoner" and the mastermind of the Seven Years (French and Indian) War, or around that connection of Whig magnates, the Saviles, the Wentworths, and Bentincks, and "the whole house of Cavendish,"[2] as Burke proudly named them, under the leadership of Charles, Marquess of Rockingham. These two general connections were by no means monolithic or politically or socially homogenous within themselves; and they were separated from each other by personal allegiances and by jealousy in the pursuit of power and leadership in the Opposition. In the rhetoric of their public policy, nevertheless, they agreed much more extensively than they disagreed; and they came so close

---

[2] Edmund Burke, *A Letter to John Farr and John Harris, Esqrs., Sheriffs of the City of Bristol, on the Affairs of America,* in *The Works of The Right Honorable Edmund Burke* (12 vols.; Boston: Little, Brown, 1894), II, 239.

to identity in their argumentative speeches and writings on American policy, that we may freely lament, at this distance and from this side of the water, that the leadership in the two connections felt it necessary to manufacture differences, even on America, to prevent effective coalition. The distaste of Burke for Chatham, for example, and of many persons for Chatham's ally Shelburne, sometimes seems in fact to be living still among the historians of the age of George III.

Now in order to enliven these matters of context and the broad generalizations which I have hazarded, let us attend to certain of the voices in action. I introduce first an adherent of Chatham and Shelburne, their ever-ready spokesman in the House of Commons, who is amply commemorated in the place names of the Northeast. He is certainly not among the most illustrious defenders of America in Parliament. His contemporaries would probably have agreed, however, that he was the most picturesque, persistent, and pugnacious of the lot; and he was in the vanguard, and almost alone in the vanguard, of the rhetorical action for America.

Colonel Isaac Barré,[3] for the greater part of his thirty years in the House of Commons, was in debate—and probably in person—the most conspicuous of those military and naval officers whom the British governmental system of the eighteenth century accepted readily into politics and Parliament. Like officers of higher rank such as General Henry Seymour Conway, Admiral Augustus Keppel, Lord Clive of India, and "Gentleman Johnny" Burgoyne, Barré returned from his compaigns in the wars for the empire to plunge into politics

---

[3] There is no considerable biography of Barré available. The most recent brief sketch is Peter Brown's in *The Chathamites* (New York: St. Martin's Press, 1967), 189–227. For some discussion of Barré as speaker, see Donald C. Bryant, "Colonel Isaac Barré—Cossack of the Opposition: The Opening of his Career," *Quarterly Journal of Speech*, XXX (1944), 55–64; and " 'A Scarecrow of Violence': Colonel Isaac Barré in the House of Commons," *Speech Monographs*, XXVIII (1961), 233–49.

at Westminster without shedding either his military rank, his military ambitions, or his soldierly temperament. Unlike his closest friend and political patron, the young Earl of Shelburne, and many another young nobleman and gentleman, Barré had not turned to the army as a temporary avocation to find prestige, friends, and adventure, or to improve his social and political position. These advantages came Barré's way, but they came to a professional officer who had left the strictly military life only after his ambitions had been frustrated and his best hopes for promotion apparently destroyed on the Plains of Abraham.

Barré's political career was analogous to his military career and was an extension of it. Qualities very like those which he exhibited as he began to earn distinction in the army brought him, not to the first, but certainly to the second order of eminence in the House of Commons.

After more than ten years of slow promotion in the military establishment, Barré came to the attention of the officer whom Pitt had seized upon to join Jeffrey Amherst in finishing the Seven Years War in America, General James Wolfe. Wolfe took him on the expedition to Louisburg in 1758 and the next year made him adjutant for the campaign against Quebec. Between campaigns Barré spent the winter with Amherst in Boston organizing American support, an experience which he would afterwards draw upon for credibility in debate. Wolfe's death at Quebec and a musket ball in Barré's own cheek which he carried for the rest of his life, sent him in disappointment back to England. There he quarreled with the War Department, and there the Earl of Shelburne took him into politics under his command. In this second phase of his national service, Barré, who was always the adjutant rather than the strategist or field commander, extended rapidly in the corps of Shelburne and Pitt those qualities which had secured for him the friendship and trust of Wolfe. In addition, the talent for combat, for which he appears never to have found sufficient scope in his military positions of subaltern and administrative officer, flourished under the political generals and made him a man to be reckoned with in the committees and on the floor of the House of Commons and in the debates in the Court of Proprietors of the East India Company. During the administrations of "Stamp Act" Grenville and Lord North, hardly a more dangerous debater could rise from the benches of the House.

I said that Barré was in the vanguard of the voices for America, for his was the only notable voice against the passage of the Stamp Act of 1765. He had sat in the Commons for three years, first as Pitt's antagonist and counterpart in invective, but shortly, along with Shelburne, Pitt's permanent ally. In February, 1765, that inveterate letter-writer and political gossip par excellence, Horace Walpole, son of the great Sir Robert, wrote to a friend in Paris: "There has been nothing of note in Parliament but one slight day on the American taxes, which, Charles Townshend supporting, received a pretty heavy thump from Barré, who is the present Pitt, and the dread of all the vociferous Norths and Rigbys, on whose lungs, depended so much of Mr. Grenville's power. Do you never hear them to Paris?"[4]

That "slight day" was the day of the passage of the Stamp Act. That violently explosive act passed with the height of indifference in the British public and went through the House "not with a bang but a whimper." Colonel Barré (Pitt being indisposed and absent) gave it its only vigorous opposition, in a speech which, through a fortuitous circumstance, made him almost as much a hero in America as some of the colonial agitators. "This Act passed the Commons almost without de-

---

[4] Mrs. Paget Toynbee (ed.), *The Letters of Horace Walpole* (16 vols.; Oxford: Clarendon Press, 1903–1905), VI, 187–88.

bate," reported Cobbett's *Parliamentary History;* "two or three members spoke against it, but without force or apparent interest, except a vehement harangue from Colonel Barré."[5] Barré's vehement harangue, however, happened to be heard and reported in America by Jared Ingersoll, agent for Connecticut,[6] and it launched a battle cry almost as popular as Patrick Henry's "Caesar had his Brutus. . . ."

Charles Townshend, who was soon to become special anathema to the Americans, closed his speech for the Stamp Act with: "These children [the Americans] of our own planting, nourished by our indulgence until they are grown to a good degree of strength and opulence, and protected by arms, will they grudge to contribute their mite to relieve us from the heavy load of national expense which we lie under?"

That set the Colonel's Pittite hostility going and roused his recollections of Americans, America, Indians, and British administrators in the colonies.

Perhaps, as Ingersoll the American reported, Barré rose "with eyes darting fire and an outstretched arm" and spoke "with a voice somewhat elevated and with a sternness in his countenance which expressed in a most lively manner the feelings of his heart." Perhaps. On the other hand, Barré himself remarked four years later, "The Stamp Act, Sir, I opposed with great good humor."[7] It is impossible to be sure precisely what the Colonel said on the floor, but what the Americans *read* that he said was entirely in character:

[5] *Ibid.*, XVI, 37.

[6] The original report of this speech appeared in the Boston *Post Boy and Advertiser* for May 27, 1765. I have taken the text from Richard Frothering-ham's transcription in *The Rise of the Republic of the United States,* (9th ed.; Boston: Little, Brown, 1905), 175, *n.* 3. The speech was reprinted, much altered, in a pamphlet, *Mr. Ingersoll's Letters Relating to the Stamp Act,* with a preface dated New Haven, June 15, 1767. That version appears to be the one which became a schoolboy declamation.

[7] John Wright (ed.), *Sir Henry Cavendish's Debates of the House of Commons* . . . (2 vols.; London: Longman, 1841–43), I, 206.

Children planted by your care? [Barré began, with dramatic incredulity] No! Your oppression planted them in
America; they fled from your tyranny to a then uncul-
tivated land, where they were exposed to almost all the
hardships to which human nature is liable, and, among
others, to the savage cruelty of the enemy of the country,
—a people, the most subtle, and, I will take upon me to say,
the most truly terrible of any people that ever inhabited
any part of GOD'S EARTH; and yet, actuated by principles of
true *English* liberty, they met all these hardships with
pleasure, compared with those they suffered in their own
country from the hands of those that should have been
their friends.

The Americans are the real Englishmen, "actuated by principles of true English liberty," ready to face hardship and terror
abroad to escape tyranny at home. Whether the ideas and
images were Barré's, or the journalist Ingersoll's, the spirit
was Barré's and the sentiments calculated very much to
please America. In the next section comes a phrase which was
picked up as a slogan by the radical resisters.

They nourished up by your indulgence? They grew by your
neglect of them. As soon as you began to take care about
them, that care was exercised in sending persons to rule
over them in one department or another, who were perhaps
the deputies of some deputy of members of this House, sent
to spy out their liberty, to misrepresent their actions, and
to prey upon them,—men whose behavior, on many occasions, has caused the blood of those Sons of LIBERTY to recoil
within them,—men promoted to the highest seats of justice:
some [of whom], to my knowledge, were glad by going to
foreign countries to escape being brought to a bar of a court
of justice in their own.

In a third and final passage, the vehement colonel speaks on
a subject on which he can justly claim special competence.

They protected by your arms? They have nobly taken up
arms in your defense, have exerted their valor, amidst their
constant and laborious industry, for the defense of a country whose frontiers, while drenched in blood, its interior

parts have yielded all its little savings to your enlargement. Barré then issued the stern warning of the second passage I quoted in opening. Then he concluded, perhaps a little histrionically, "But the subject is too delicate. I will say no more." That speech, as I have said, caused no stir in Parliament and was quietly ignored by the public outside; but it forecast the themes which the colonel and the other voices for America were to drum away at for many years to come. Barré's label, *Sons of Liberty*, though almost buried in the middle of the speech, struck the fancy of colonial agitators as the name of the most militant of their protest organizations.

William Pitt, as we might suppose, was delighted with the initiative of his lieutenant (colonel), and Shelburne wrote to Barré: "I am happy to hear of your success the American day. It must give your friends in America the greatest pleasure."[8] Indeed it did. For example, when the town of Hutchinson, Massachusetts, founded in 1774 and named after the royal governor, petitioned in 1776 to have its hated name changed to Wilkes, the General Assembly of Massachusetts chose, rather, to name it Barré.[9] Before long the two names were united in the new border town among the mountains of northern Pennsylvania.

As every young American knows—but no, that is too reckless a remark. As every young American had read or heard in the days when our colonial history was a regular, required study in the elementary schools and high schools—the passage of the Stamp Act and the attempt to collect the tax in this

[8] Lord Fitzmaurice, *Life of William Earl of Shelburne* (2nd ed., rev.; 2 vols.; London: Macmillan, 1912), I, 224–25.

[9] When the town of Barre celebrated its centennial in 1874, all the powers of oratory, poetry, and art were taxed to do honor to the colonel. A full account of these ceremonies may be found in *A Memorial of the One Hundredth Anniversary of the Town of Barre* . . . (Cambridge, Mass.: J. Wilson and Son, 1875). I have noted the highlights in "Cossack," note 3 above.

country brought to sharp focus the brewing dissatisfaction of many of the colonials and set off active resistance in the colonies north and south. It was that act which detonated Patrick Henry's legendary explosion, "Caesar had his Brutus. . . ."

The news reaching England through the spring of 1765 contributed to the fall of George Grenville, whom the king and his friends had sought cause to replace; and it helped bring into office a partially changed set of ministers of whom the Marquess of Rockingham became the leader. Pitt and his allies, who had welcomed Grenville's fall but had been unable to agree to take office themselves, could no more bring themselves to join with the Rockingham group. They, however, like the Rockinghams, were committed to the repeal of the Stamp Act and to restoring what in their public statements they called the former, unsuspecting confidence of the colonies in the Mother Country.

Barré gave way to the "Great Commoner" Pitt, who was not yet Lord Chatham, as the principal voice for America on the repeal of the Stamp Act; and on the same side Edmund Burke cut his parliamentary teeth.

The third and fourth quotations in our opening series are probably familiar as words of Pitt. The first he spoke in declaring for repeal of the Stamp Act: "I rejoice that America has resisted"; the second, demanding in the House of Lords in the midst of the war an end to the war. We'll come to that.

Pitt was a popular hero, the Great Commoner. He was, some people still think, the greatest orator England ever had. He was also a thorough *prima donna*, of measureless self-regard and self-confidence. When he took over the conduct of the French and Indian War he declared, "I know that I can save this country, and that no one else can." His scorn for concession to his opponents, and his arrogant independence enhanced his popular appeal. When he chose to speak in Parliament, perhaps following a late, well-advertised, and theatrical entrance, the galleries were crowded and other business was put aside.

Chatham's was the oratory of indignation, of harassment, of invective, and grand appeals to liberty, to patriotism, to English freedom, and the British constitution. Henry Grattan, his great Irish admirer, saw him as a highly accomplished actor playing the grand role of himself. Unlike his coequal voice for America, Edmund Burke, Chatham was not notable for close or extended argument. He relied on repeated assertion of his own assumed authority; on memorable sentences ("I contend not for indulgence, but justice for America."); on gross figures of speech ("*hell-hounds, I say, of savage war*"); on appeals to traditional British good sense. His position on every important question was awaited with eagerness or apprehension by friend and foe, and his speeches were listened to as no others were. In public speaking (though not in command of votes), Chatham was the most formidable friend of America, and on America and the problems of America he made his most famous and most often-quoted speeches.

Perhaps Chatham's refusal to join others but to expect others to join him was responsible for the difficult distinction he came to for his treatment of American taxation. In order to get the Stamp Act repealed against the wishes of the Court and its allies, the Rockingham government added the Declaratory Act reaffirming the principle that Parliament was competent to legislate for the colonies "in all things whatsoever," though declining to exercise the power in taxation. Chatham, however, chose to deny that legislation included taxing power, and thus he and his allies, including Barré, could speak in favor of repeal of the Stamp Act while withholding their support from the administration which was staking its life on that repeal.

Hence in the debates opening the Parliament of 1766,

which was to repeal the Stamp Act, the Great Commoner
could declare in his grandest tones:

> Gentlemen, Sir, have been charged with giving birth to
> *sedition* in America. [Senator Fulbright and others, we re-
> call, have been charged with giving hope and strength to
> the Viet Cong and the North Vietnamese.] Several have
> spoken their sentiments with freedom against this un-
> happy act, and that freedom has become their crime. Sorry
> I am to hear the liberty of speech in this House imputed as
> a crime. But the imputation shall not discourage me. It is
> liberty I mean to exercise. . . . The Gentleman tells us,
> America is obstinate; America is almost in open rebellion.
> I rejoice that America has resisted. Three millions of peo-
> ple, so dead to all the feelings of liberty as voluntarily to
> submit to be slaves, would have been fit instruments to
> make slaves of the rest. . . . [He demanded] that the Stamp
> Act be *repealed absolutely, totally,* and *immediately.* That
> the reason for the repeal be assigned, because it was
> founded upon an erroneous principle. At the same time let
> the sovereign authority of this country over the colonies be
> asserted in as strong terms as can be devised.[10]

Liberty of speech, resistance to the threat of slavery, removal
of illegitimate taxation, but governing still with full authority
—these are sure-fire appeals, especially from a Pitt. Then the
great voice for America, seeking, it would seem, to pull the rug
from under the Rockingham voices by disowning the Declaratory Act, concluded "and be made to extend to every point of
legislation whatsoever, except that of taking their money out
of their pockets without their consent." Thus Pitt, Chatham-
to-be, joined in the American cry that taxation without representation is tyranny, to the discredit of those who were
actually removing the taxation. Not much more than a year
later Chatham's own administration, which succeeded the
Rockingham "repeal" administration, levied the Townshend
duties on the colonies and started the trouble all over again,

[10] Francis Thackery, *A History of the Right Honourable William Pitt, Earl
of Chatham, Containing his Speeches in Parliament* . . . (2 vols.; London:
Printed for C. and J. Rivington, 1827), II, 69-72.

right or no right. The great voice, to be sure, had lapsed into one of his celebrated psychic illnesses and had lost control of his ill-assorted colleagues.

Through the first half of the seventies, however, and on after the war finally came, during the ministry of Lord North, Chatham and Shelburne in the House of Lords and their voices in the Commons, principally Barré, fought for the Americans on almost all occasions. They often managed to put aside their antagonism to the Rockinghams, and on American matters at least, made a chorus of voices in seeming harmony.

It is one thing, of course, to oppose the steps and actions leading to war. It is another, as we know, to demand negotiated peace after the fighting has begun and the country is committed to military victory. The penalities for the latter are greater; but Chatham and Barré on the one hand, and the Rockinghams and their eminent voice, Edmund Burke, on the other, sustained the campaign through all.

Three months before Lexington and Concord, Chatham demanded the removal of the British troops from Boston and declared, "This glorious spirit of Whiggism animates three millions in America; who prefer poverty with liberty, to gilded chains and sordid affluence; and who will die in defense of their rights as men, as freemen."[11] Almost three years later, just before news of Saratoga arrived, the voice, though near its final silence, was strong and unyielding still:

> I love and honor the English troops: I know their virtues and their valor: I' know they can achieve anything except impossibilities: and I know that the conquest of English America *is an impossibility.* You cannot, I venture to say it, you CANNOT conquer America. . . . [and then the fourth quotation from our opening series] If I were an American, as I am an Englishman, while a foreign troop was landed

[11] *Ibid.*, II, 286. January 20, 1775.

in my country, I would never lay down my arms—never—never—never.[12]

In this same speech Chatham gave final expression to the second point on which he differed from the other voices for America. As eager as he was to end the war and reconcile the colonies and England, and ready as he was to make almost any concession, he was too much the proud architect of the empire to admit independence for America into the price. Burke, Fox, and the Rockinghams, who never *formally* abandoned the right of taxation, sadly agreed, as Burke wrote in 1777, that independence without war was to be preferred to independence through war.[13]

The British voice for America most widely known in this country and most carefully read over the years—the one also with whom literate Britons are probably most familiar—was Edmund Burke. I have, I know, already devoted a whole essay to Burke, and I shall turn to one of his major efforts on American affairs next. Even so one cannot honestly leave him out of a gallery of the major rhetorical friends of our forefathers the English in the colonies. Burke's, I scarcely need to remind you, are the words of the first quotation with which we began, from the famous speech of March, 1775, *On Conciliation with the Colonies.* We shall return to it shortly.

Like Barré, Burke, we recall, was born, reared, and educated in Ireland, where he trained himself well in literary and rhetorical activities, with special emphasis on history. Before he entered Parliament at the age of thirty-seven, his American studies were well under way. He early intended to migrate to America, but though he never came to this continent, as Colonel Barré had, he made himself more fully and better

[12] *Ibid.,* II, 326–27. November 18, 1777.
[13] Burke, *Letter to the Sheriffs of Bristol,* in *Works,* II, 236.

acquainted with America than any other public man of his time. "I think I know America," Burke wrote in 1777, "—if I do not, my ignorance is incurable, for I have spared no pains to understand it."[14]

Burke began his American studies in the 1750s by collaborating with a relative on a history of the *European Settlements in America* (1757), in two volumes of over six hundred pages. In the late 1750s also, as I have pointed out, he began writing the *Annual Register*, for which each year to the mid-1760s he composed the long history of the year in England and abroad. To equip himself he read prodigiously and attended Parliament as regularly as permitted. His experience in the active politics of American affairs began immediately upon his securing the position of private secretary to the Marquess of Rockingham in July of 1765. He was given a seat in the House of Commons the following January and was the Marquess' invaluable agent in helping secure the repeal of the Stamp Act. As we know, Burke made his first parliamentary speeches during the debates preceding the repeal, but of course his was not the major voice it was to become in a very short time. Nevertheless, Chatham condescended to praise him.

Like most of the other voices after 1766, Burke's sounded from the benches of the Opposition in Parliament, but his voice went out powerfully also through the press.

In a sense, the culmination of the first phase of Burke's continuous campaign for America was his election to Parliament for the large commercial city of Bristol in 1774. That spring, in debate on the repeal of the American tea duty, the last of the Townshend taxes, Burke had reviewed the whole vast question of American relations and the men responsible for them, and had come out strongly for the repeal. Repeal, of

[14] *Ibid.*, 209.

course, failed, but for the record and for the furtherance of the cause outside the House, Burke published the speech from the shorthand notes of Sir Henry Cavendish. That, the *Speech on American Taxation*, was the first of Burke's three major published pieces on American affairs. This one appeared while there still seemed time to avert conflict by returning to the old system, and Burke as the conspicuous and sanguine advocate of concession and commerce, seemed to the principal merchants and traders of Bristol to be just their man. Besides that, Burke was the parliamentary agent for the Assembly of the Colony of New York.

Burke's second major work in Parliament and the press, about a year later, came when the voices for America in Britain still had not given up all hope of a peaceful settlement, but when events were just passing the breaking point. It was the *Speech on Conciliation*, with which Burke introduced into the Commons his six resolutions for removing the obstructions to reconciliation and for taking positive actions toward a new relationship. I shall not quote extensively from that speech, though it is eminently quotable. The first of my opening quotations is one of the most permanently wise and eloquent passages from it: "The proposition is Peace."[15] You will recall also Burke's fine characterization of the energy, the venturesomeness, the enterprise of the Americans—their incredible capacity for what we might now call "population growth," and their indomitable devotion to their precious inheritance of English liberty. ("An Englishman is the unlikeliest person in the world to argue another Englishman into slavery.") You will remember Burke's eloquent expositions of the wise and the possible in the government of free people and of wide empire. ("I do not know the method of drawing up an indictment against an whole people." "A great empire and little

[15] *Ibid.*, 105–106.

minds go ill together.") Contrary to the expectation of the
public, Burke bypassed altogether the divisive question of the
right of taxation ("It is not what a lawyer tells me I *may* do;
but what humanity, justice, and reason tell me I ought to do
[that is the question]"). Burke's resolutions, supported also by
the talented new recruit to the cause, Charles James Fox,
"with the greatest ability and spirit,"[16] of course failed. In
November, after news of Lexington and Concord, the "shot
heard round the world," and after Henry's vehement embrac-
ing of liberty or death, Burke spoke again in Parliament for
conciliation, and that time explicitly abandoned claim of the
right of taxation. Burke did not publish that second speech,
probably realizing that the controversy was, in effect, dead for
the time. The speech, however, judging by the reports and by
Burke's notes which remain, established him as one who
would stay with the cause after the commitment to war had
seized the Government and the public.

Burke's *Speech on Conciliation with America* occupies a
special kind of place in the Anglo-American cultural inheritance. In England, like the *Speech on American Taxation*, it
went through repeated editions in the later 1770s, but in the
long run it was pushed into the background of interest by
Burke's *Reflections on the Revolution in France*, a subject and
a danger which shook Englishmen much more violently and
directly than the loss of America.

In America *On Conciliation* was published in New York in
1775, and after independence it appeared honorably in anthologies and collections of great orations, such as the Yale
professor Chauncey Goodrich's *Select British Eloquence* in
1852. Fine as the speech was, and quotable by innumerable
speakers and writers for its practical, political wisdom, it did

---

[16] Loren Reid, *Charles James Fox: A Man for the People* (Columbia, Mo.:
University of Missouri Press, 1969), 56.

not embody the quality of simple harangue that made Barré's Sons of Liberty speech a favorite of schoolboy declaimers and fitted it for versification for patriotic celebrations.[17] Beginning in the 1890s, however, an educated American could hardly have become so without grappling seriously with Edmund Burke *On Conciliation.* For about half a century, including the time when I was a schoolboy, and even later, detailed study of that speech was a required part of the senior high-school English course.

I will not undertake to account for this belated adoption of the distinguished speech of the distinguished voice for America as the climax of literary-historical education for the great majority of Americans. No doubt it fitted into the educational philosophy of our grandfathers, and not without good reason. Of Burke's published speeches, that one is the most obviously preplanned and carefully constructed in a familiar pseudo-classical pattern. It exhibits most of the characteristics of composition which teachers of English would have been happy to have their students approximate. Many of Burke's paragraphs, for example, actually have topic sentences and develop them. And of course in its substance that speech called the attention of those generations of young Americans to an aspect of our inheritance to which I am recalling attention.

In his lively new biography of Burke's friend Charles James Fox, Loren Reid indulges in a brief, amusing side excursion, in which he observes: "The total influence of this nationwide ingestion of Burke—in city schools and in rural districts—has never been explored. . . . Young Americans memorized excerpts from their own orators, Webster, Lincoln, Ingersoll, and others, but they *chewed, swallowed,* and *digested*

---

[17] See note 9, above.

Burke."[18] The fact remains, therefore, that of the conspicuous voices for America, Burke's is the only one whom a considerable number of Americans have heard, and not just heard of.

Such were the sounds and the basic messages of some of the major friendly voices focused upon America before and during the War of Independence. Of course, there were many other such voices, some of which I have mentioned in passing. By 1774, for example, and on through the peace of 1783, the remarkable Charles James Fox was a powerful spokesman for America both on his own and in support of Burke. The fifth quotation of our opening galaxy[19] was spoken by him in 1774 at the outset of his involvement, and by the time which I shall treat in my next lecture, he was a major debater in the cause. Besides Chatham in the House of Lords, the Earl of Shelburne and the Duke of Richmond spoke for America. In public, perhaps Shelburne was more important for sustaining Colonel Barré and for promoting Richard Price than for raising his own voice.

Price, the author of the last quotation in our opening anthology, was a religious Dissenter who, with that other famous Dissenter, Joseph Priestley, was a member of Shelburne's coterie of political and social liberals, libertarians, and reformers. Characteristically of Dissenters, Price raised his voice for America, incidentally to his other causes; and early in 1776 he published his *Observations on the Nature of Civil Liberty and the Justice and Policy of the War with America.* From that pamphlet comes our quotation.[20]

For the most part the established clergy, the clergy of the Church of England, supported the war and the punishment—

[18] Reid, *Charles James Fox*, 57.
[19] William Cobbett (ed.), *Parliamentary History of England* (36 vols.; London: Bagshaw, 1806–1820), XVII, 1313.
[20] The passage is included in Max Beloff (ed.), *The Debate on the American Revolution* (London: Nicholas Kaye, 1949), 269–70.

and thus presumably the redemption—of the rebels. Sad to say, John Wesley, the voice of the Methodists, in spite of his experience in Georgia, took the same anti-American position. An exception among the Anglicans was the maverick Bishop Shipley of the Welsh diocese of St. Asaphs. Shipley was an independent liberal who was also a member of Shelburne's circle. He preached in his cathedral against the American War, he advocated parliamentary reform, and he supported relief for dissenters. In 1774 he published a speech, "intended to have been spoken" by him in the House of Lords, against the bills called in America the Intolerable Acts. The speech was reprinted in Philadelphia, and Jefferson's copy with Shipley's name on it in Jefferson's hand is extant.[21] Why he had not delivered it is unknown. Perhaps he never intended to deliver it, but used the fiction of the parliamentary speech as a plausible vehicle for direct, unpretentious popular address. Perhaps also a sense of futility, which he confesses in the text, played a part. As a pamphlet, the speech would serve to widen the currency, in both Britain and America, of the Burkean-Chathamite theme of moderation, friendship, and conciliation for mutual benefit and happiness. In concluding Shipley writes: "My Lords, I have ventured to lay my thoughts before you, on the greatest national concern that ever came under your deliberation . . . with a melancholy assurance, that not a word of it will be regarded. And yet, my Lords," he continues, "with your permission, I will waste one short argument more on the same cause, one that I own I am fond of, and which contains in it, what, I think, must affect every generous mind. My Lords, I look upon North America as the only great

---

[21] *A Speech Intended to have been Spoken on the Bill for Altering the Charters of the Colony of Massachusett's Bay* (3rd ed.; London, Printed: Philadelphia: Reprinted and sold by William and Thomas Bradford, 1774). See Charles Evans, *American Bibliography: A Chronological Dictionary* . . . (14 vols.; Chicago: printed for the author, 1903–1959), V, item 13620.

nursery of freemen now left upon the face of the earth." Jefferson would be unlikely to dissent.

The voices of moderation, of conciliation, of plain goodwill, no matter how eloquent—the voices of peace without victory —seldom prevail, as we know all too well, in the atmosphere and context of violence and force until events conspire with voices to demonstrate the futility of continuing the fight. Until Yorktown in 1781, the great voices for America, and the less great, could keep the cause alive, could get Englishmen used to the idea of independence for America, and could prepare themselves for the day when they should come to power; but only with news of Cornwallis' surrender came the final conviction of people and Court that a new relationship was necessary. Persistent voices for a good cause are always essential, but are seldom—or never—enough. They reinforce and interpret events, and from events they draw the ultimate impulse of their power.

V

The Rhetorical Art of Edmund Burke
A Letter to the Sheriffs of Bristol, 1777

Now, as I forecast, we return to Edmund Burke and to his rhetorical art as it may be examined, not in extemporaneous debate or in those pamphlets representing speeches made in Parliament or on the hustings, but in a work intended from its inception for a reading audience primarily outside Parliament. We shall examine what seem to me the principal rhetorical strategies and the dominant stylistic features operating in Burke's *Letter to the Sheriffs of Bristol* (1777).[1] The *Letter* is the third and last of that celebrated trio of publications, beginning with the *Speech on American Taxation* of 1774, through which Burke sought to avert the war with America or to stop it after it had started. As I treat the *Letter*, perhaps I shall be able to exhibit in flesh and blood, so to speak, various aspects of what I earlier called rhetorical dimensions in criticism.

After the fighting of the war had got seriously under way, after Washington had been given command of an American army, after the Declaration of Independence had been signed

---

[1] *A Letter to John Farr and John Harris, Esqrs., Sheriffs of the City of Bristol, on the Affairs of America*, in *The Works of the Right Honorable Edmund Burke* (12 vols.; Boston: Little, Brown, 1894), II, 189–245. Citations of this work will appear hereafter as page numbers in parentheses in the text.

and news of it spread in England, and especially after news of Howe's victories of 1776 near New York, enthusiasm for the war ran high in England. In consequence Burke and the other friends of America came more intensely than before to be branded as voices of treason and not of merely bothersome, misguided Opposition.

At this low point in the cause of peace, with congratulatory resolutions flooding to the king from municipal corporations all over the land, with even pulpits sounding bloody condemnation of the "rebels," Burke and his friends found themselves unable to participate in the elation at the news of English victories and the prospect of the defeat of the colonies. On the other hand, they could do nothing to damp the enthusiasm or to reverse or modify the policies and practices with which North's government was prosecuting the war.

For a period they seceded from Parliament in protest, thus calling special attention to their refusal to be party to iniquities which they were helpless to prevent. On the other hand, they proved unable to agree, though they tried several times, upon a group statement or party manifesto on American affairs.[2] Burke, therefore, in his own name as Member for Bristol, but with the concurrence of his major party colleagues, addressed the public through an open letter to the sheriffs. He chose the sheriffs rather than the mayor or the corporation because he knew the sheriffs to be friendly to his position, whereas the mayor had been conspicuous in congratulatory addresses to the king on Howe's victories in America. Intended initially as a justification of his party's absenting itself from Parliament in protest against the vi-

---

[2] In late 1776 Burke composed and submitted to Rockingham and their colleagues two separate statements, neither of which was actually issued by the party. The composition of these papers, an *Address to the King* and an *Address to the British Colonists in North America*, contributed much to the *Letter to the Sheriffs, Works*, VI, 151–96.

cious, punitive bills for Letters of Marque and Reprisal and suspension of *habeas corpus* in cases of alleged treason committed in the colonies or on the high seas, the *Letter* turned, as Burke's speeches and writings almost always turned, into something much larger—a comprehensive indictment of British policy and action on America since the repeal of the Stamp Act.

The common literary and journalistic vehicle of the letter provided for Burke in the circumstances certain tactical and psychological advantages. First of all and basically it permitted him to assume the rhetorical posture of advising with persons already sympathetic to his position, persons sharing his detestation of the American War and the ministerial policy responsible for it—that is, persons not requiring to be convinced or converted. Secondly, at the same time that the publication functioned as a manifesto for the Rockinghams, the posture of writing a letter to friends and political sympathizers enabled Burke to speak for his colleagues without binding any but himself, and made it easy for him to praise them as they could not decently praise themselves. In the third place, the freedom of the letter form made it plausible for Burke to begin officially and conventionally with a member of Parliament's formal transmittal to his constituents of copies of two recent acts of Parliament, to dilate on the unhappy implications of those acts, and then to lengthen and deepen the formality into a free and total indictment of the policy of which the acts were the latest vicious expression.

Artistically the letter invited the idiom of direct address, like a speech, and it established the propriety of personal reference and unembarrassed talk of oneself. At the same time it freely permitted exposition and argument in the third person. It enabled Burke to dispense with conventional development but still to build as full a case as he wished, to escape requirements or expectations of obvious structural conventions and to rove freely among subjects and moods which circumstances, persons, and the state of the controversy invited. He was not required to prove; he could freely exhort and indict.

Unlike his previous publications on American policy, Burke's *Letter to the Sheriffs of Bristol* is not primarily a work of evidential advocacy or demonstrative argument. It is predominantly a venture in declarative indictment. Burke's readers, he assumes, are generally conscious enough of events and popular attitudes and opinions to require only allusions to events and reminders of circumstances upon which he will ground interpretive assertions. Burke brings evidence to bear certainly: the provisions of the new act suspending *habeas corpus;* the employment of Hessians and Indians by the British commanders; the statement of the Continental Congress that after the repeal of the Stamp Act "the colonies fell into their ancient state of unsuspecting confidence in the mother country" (234). The explicit evidence, however, is infrequent, serving chiefly to illustrate and reinforce declarations about national policy and public morality and behavior. Such tactic is in harmony with the stance of the patriotic, humane statesman addressing a sympathetic audience in moral indictment of a policy and a ministry with which the audience is familiar. This is a proper tactic also for a counterpart justification of one's own position and conduct and the position and conduct of one's colleagues and associates, with which also the readers have been familiar over an extended time. Even in transmitting to his constituents the two new oppressive acts, Burke spends little space in delineating facts and events—which were there for all to observe. He himself has previously dealt with them at length in the House and in print. The meaning of facts and events; the consequences of them; the significance for the health of British society, for the welfare of the empire, and for the preservation of free government—these are for

Burke the issues which demand forceful, popular interpretation quite different from that most generally abroad in Bristol and in the land.

A plausible and organic sequence of ideas—of *matters* of indictment—stands out clearly. The *Letter* progresses from faults of the immediate acts and the dangerous implications of them for British liberty and British society, to the larger issues of policy and action of which they are lamentable parts and consequences, both at home and in America. It exposes the mistaken, potentially catastrophic, principles of policy with respect to America and to dissent and opposition at home, on which the prosecution of the American War is conducted. It reiterates a brief history of the misconceived and misguided progress of events in consequence of those principles. And finally it reasserts the conciliating principles of wise and prudent government, which, Burke declares, might have forestalled trouble in the first place, and could still, he thinks, salvage something good from the mounting wreckage, both at home and abroad. A plausible conclusion to the indictment is Burke's apologia for his own actions and the actions of his friends over a period of a decade, and his exhortation to the faithful to be firm for a salutary policy of reconciliation and healing.

Such in brief is the master pattern of the whole. No one, I think, would venture to see in Burke's *Letter* the structure of the classical oration which critics have sought to identify in detail in the speech *On Conciliation.* The *Letter,* as I have observed, is a letter, like Burke's *Reflections on the Revolution in France* and his famous *Letter to a Noble Lord.* It grows, it enlarges, from discussion of particular, immediate concerns to more and more expanded treatment of antecedent and related factors—sometimes in digressions, sometimes in backtracks and retrospect, sometimes in assault, sometimes defense, always, however, generating a sense of coherence, of relevance, if not of structural tidiness and unity. The specifics of the indictment as they emerge and recur become together a virtual inventory of the consequences of Government policy upon which Opposition could freely vent its condemnation:

(1) The wickedness of a war of arms and laws against brethren;

(2) The charge that the Americans are traitors and rebels;

(3) The impolicy and injustice of a civil war—Englishmen in the home islands against Englishmen in America;

(4) The denial of English constitutional liberties abroad, which would not be tolerated at home;

(5) The delusion that a revenue could be gained from America by force of arms;

(6) The stupidity of trying to subdue America by force as a way to accommodation and reconciliation;

(7) The horrible barbarity of employing German mercenaries and savage Indians against one's kinsmen and children;

(8) The folly of abusing and insulting the Americans *en masse*—of drawing up "an indictment against an whole people"—and of whipping up passion against kinsmen as a means of redeeming them;

(9) The political folly of enforcing abstract principles and theoretical powers in government against the sense of the community to be governed;

(10) The absence of lenity, moderation, restraint, and plain goodwill in the government of a wide empire;

(11) The berating of honest, patriotic dissent at home and treating sympathy for Americans as equivalent to treason;

(12) The deterioration and corruption of English law, English manners, and English freedom everywhere through the use of unconstitutional and impolitic

means of subduing the English in America;

(13) The corrupt domination of Parliament by an evil ministry, and the shameful abdication by Parliament of
its primary duty of serving and defending the people.

The force and meaning of the indictment build up more
significantly through the persistent refrains and intertwined
and reinforced themes than through logical progress of topics
and argument. Style and texture—the form, movement, and
management of language—carry the burden of the message
and give it its power.

Striking, memorable statements of traditional English
principles and the ancient English spirit of freedom and or-
dered liberty furnish the staple of the message. This staple,
Burke enlarges and deepens by profuse interweaving of aphoristic and sententious observations on human nature and the
natural, characteristic behavior of men in society and in government.

Nowhere in the *Letter*, for example, does there appear a
sustained passage condemning the use of Hessians and Indians in the war. Burke was to set that horror in its strongest
light the following year in his celebrated speech of February
6 in the House of Commons, moving for papers on the military
employment of Indians in America.[3] The theme, nevertheless,
pierces the *Letter* again and again sharpening the feeling for
abused Englishmen, "kinsmen," in the colonies. It is a recur-

---

[3] Horace Walpole entered in his *Journals*: "The 6th was memorable for the
chef-d'oeuvre of Burke's orations. . . . *He drew iron tears* down Barré's cheek,
who implored him to print his speech, and said, with many invectives against
the Bishops, that it ought to be pasted up on every church under *their* procla-
mation of the Fast, and that he himself would paste it up-on some." A. Francis
Steuart (ed.), *The Last Journals of Horace Walpole During the Reign of George
III, 1771–1783* (2 vols.; London: Lane, 1910), II, 104. Summary texts of the
three-and-a-half-hour speech may be found in William Cobbett (ed.), *Parliamentary History of England* (36 vols.; London: Bagshaw, 1806–1820), XIX,
694–99; and in Burke's collected *Speeches* (4 vols.; London: Longman, Hurst
et al., 1816), I, 393–400.

rent vehicle for condemnation of the "unnatural" war and of the cynicism and inhumanity of those interests conducting the war in America and supporting it in England.

The theme of the Hessians would arouse in some readers the ordinary Englishman's latent jealousy of the German connections of the royal family, in others their general hostility to foreigners, and in most the capacity for horror at brutality practiced against fellow countrymen. Burke introduces the German mercenaries casually, early in the *Letter*. He remarks, "War is at present carried on between the king's natural and foreign troops, on one side, and the English in America, on the other, upon the usual footing of other wars" (195). This sentence connects a theme already well established, that the so-called rebels are Englishmen—"the English in the colonies," "the English on the continent," "our brethren" (189)—with the theme of foreign mercenaries. A few pages later we read of the "liberal government of this free nation . . . supported by the hireling sword of German boors and vassals" so that the colonists seek protection for their "English privileges" in the arms of that prime foreign enemy, France (204). Here the appeal to sentiment hostile to the crown's German connections becomes more open. And the ever-ready fear and jealousy of France add a telling thrust.

In the next paragraph Burke intertwines still more tightly the opposing themes of English kinsmen and foreigner. In the *Court Gazette*, he says, he reads of the English-Hessian victories near New York. But, he writes in his prevailing tone of understatement:

> It is not instantly that I can be brought to rejoice, when I hear of the slaughter and captivity of long lists of those names which have been familiar to my ears from my infancy, and to rejoice that they have fallen under the sword of strangers, whose barbarous appellations I scarcely know how to pronounce. The glory acquired at White Plains by Colonel Rahl has no charms for me, and I fairly acknowl-

edge that I have not yet learned to delight in finding Fort Kniphausen in the heart of the British dominions (204).

This passage is as near to humor—sad and ironic, to be sure —as Burke ever comes in the *Letter.* The Americans have names familiar from childhood; the Germans, "barbarous appellations." The juxtaposition of the pure English "White Plains" and the German "Rahl" points the "unnaturalness" very directly, and many of Burke's readers would know that after the good English Fort Washington, above New York, had been taken from the Americans, it had been renamed for General Knyphausen, who had captured it.

As Burke paints the deplorable state of British affairs, he continues to exploit the provocation of the foreign soldier: "Those gentlemen who have prayed for war . . . and their German allies of twenty hireling states" assault "the unprepared strength of our own infant colonies" (205); they "offer their own persons" but "are satisfied with hiring Germans"; they cheer "when the unfeeling arm of a foreign soldiery pours out their kindred blood like water" (207). The "old partiality to the English name," Burke declares, "is a thousand times more worth to us than the mercenary zeal of all the circles of Germany" (208).

Whatever the particular context, Burke's pervasive theme —his prevailing image—is Americans as "kindred," as Englishmen. He makes no point in the *Letter* of demonstrating the old English spirit and blood in the Americans, as he had done at length in the speech-pamphlet *On Conciliation.* He assumes it and plays the theme into the text as a sustaining tone again and again, broken with the jarring note of the brutal, insensitive foreigner. Given all the support the "leaders of this war" cry for, he says for example, "they could not hire one German more than they do, or inspire him with less feeling for the persons or less value for the privileges of their revolted brethren" (215).

As his indictment grows more severe, his horror at the war more intense, his frustration more painful, finally he heaps Indians upon Germans. For enlisting the savage allies, he observes bitterly, there is not even the excuse of gratifying the Germans at court. Referring to those who condemn dissent at home, Burke writes: "If we all adopted their sentiments to a man, their allies, the savage Indians, could not be more ferocious than they are: they could not murder one more helpless woman or child, or with more exquisite refinements of cruelty torment to death one more of their English flesh and blood, than they do already" (215). Should there be a recognized "American party" in England, the Americans could turn to that party for support and would not "be driven to seek for protection against the fury of foreign mercenaries and the waste of savages in the arms of France" (216).

In the strategy and development of the *Letter* it is evident, as we have seen, that the sustaining theme is the concept of the colonists as aggrieved and abused Englishmen resisting oppression in arms. That concept colors and commands all else. The Americans are not criminals, rebels, pirates, or revolting vassals; they are honorable opponents in a civil war which has been forced upon them. The effect of that concept is to raise the status of the American War from a refractory disturbance of disaffected subjects—to be put down by force and concluded only by unconditional submission—into a civil war to be settled by accommodation and reconciliation. Invoking at one point the idiom and atmosphere of domestic legal dispute, he insists that "it is not by deciding the suit, but by compromising the difference, that peace can be restored or kept" (231). Unless sober, judicious readers comprehend the basic difference between the American resistance and ordinary rebellion, they will think it unreasonable to oppose measures for subduing the colonies by destroying them. "Whenever a rebellion really and truly exists," Burke declares, it "is as easily known in fact as it is difficult to define in words" (196). The American War is not of that sort, he insists, and must not be conducted as if it were. For this reason especially the use of German mercenaries and savage Indians is lamentable.

The intertwined themes of Englishmen—kinsmen in the colonies—and the Germans and Indians slaughtering them could work powerfully to enhance a sense of justified civil war, if anything could, in all but the hard-core militants. The task is difficult, as Americans know by experience of the war of 1861–1865. For years, many northerners called it the War of the Rebellion, to be ended with submission and punishment. Lincoln did not so conceive it, and had he lived he might have managed to "bind up this nation's wounds." Now at least it is normal to speak, in the spirit of Lincoln, of the War between the States, or the Civil War.

To such a distinction Burke strove to give reality and vitality in the heat and passion of the event and the exultation of apparent victory. Though he could hardly expect a transformation in his opponents, he could foster in the potentially sympathetic part of the public a feeling which might one day overcome the fanatics for war and make a peaceful accommodation possible.

Toward the conclusion of the *Letter*, Burke acknowledges to his correspondents a certain strong emotional tone in his discourse. "I feel warmly on this subject," he writes, "and I express myself as I feel" (237). Indeed Burke does express himself "warmly"; and given the situation and the substance and the object of his indictment, it would have seemed incongruous for him to behave otherwise.

Within the first two pages we read of the deep "malignity" of the act suspending *habeas corpus* (190) and of the "ignominious punishments" it prescribes to "execute vengeance" on the so-called "pirates" (190). We witness the treatment of an accused American, who "is brought hither in the dungeon of a ship's hold; thence he is vomited into a dungeon on land, loaded with irons," and at last "executed according to form" but not "tried according to justice" (192–93). Such sharply worded, balanced antithesis is one of Burke's characteristic vehicles for ending a paragraph with memorable force, or pointing the conclusion of an image. Again, it is surely a strange "idea of English dignity," he declares, "to think the defeats in America compensated by the triumphs at Tyburn" (193). The latent passion in the ironic juncture of "triumph" and the gallows at "Tyburn" would not escape Burke's readers—especially, perhaps, those who had responded to the irony of *Letters of Junius.*

The "warmth" of feeling is evident from the opening pages, but in keeping with the appropriate strategy of reasonable discourse to sober men, it grows in intensity gradually, as the first half of the *Letter* develops and the readers are acclimated to feeling.

We have already observed the increasing heat in terms and manner with which Burke sounds the theme of Germans and Indians. After the ironic passage on the "barbarous appellations" of Colonel Rahl and Fort Knyphausen (204), he loosens a little the rein he has kept upon his passion and he builds to a minor burst of indignation against reckless and ignorant proponents of violence. He speaks of their "presumptuous ignorance . . . directed by insolent passion," and concludes:

> I cannot conceive any existence under heaven (which in the depths of its wisdom tolerates all sorts of things) that is more truly odious and disgusting than an impotent, helpless creature, without civil wisdom or military skill, without a consciousness of any other qualification for power but his servility to it, bloated with pride and arrogance, calling for battles which he is not to fight, contending for a violent dominion which he can never exercise, and satisfied to be himself mean and miserable, in order to render others contemptible and wretched (206).

Burke's talent for the strong language of polemic will sometimes lead him to more savage and ingenious vituperation,
but in its way this does very well.

Immediately following that "warm" declamation, Burke re-
turns by contrast to quiet, sober language through which the
Letter generates a sense of control and restraint accentuating
the contrast between the fanatics of war and tyranny on the
one hand, and on the other Burke himself and his correspondents—those haters of civil war, those lovers of moderation,
lenity, and reconciliation, those adherents to the ancient English constitutional principles of freedom and good sense.

Other elements in the style of the *Letter*—in the management of language—operate, in a measure deliberately on
Burke's part it seems, to achieve the tone of restraint, of
reasonableness, or at least of thoughtfulness. Contributing
subtly to that tone are Burke's recurrent understatement and
irony in the expression of feeling. He hopes, for example, that
because of his unwillingness to go along with the congratula-
tion to the throne over the American victories, his correspondents will not "have the worse opinion of me for my declining
to participate in this joy" (204). Condemning "presumptuous
ignorance" and "insolent passion," he observes that "a con-
scientious man would be cautious how he dealt in blood" (206).

Contributing further to the sense of reasonableness governing passion in the texture of the *Letter* is, of course, the dominant movement of sentences, which works to screen and
mitigate what otherwise might seem extravagance of language. Critics of prose discourse have traditionally observed
the stabilizing effects of rhythmic periods, of balance and antithesis, which help give a special tone to much eighteenth-
century English literary prose. Those elements—the doublets
and triplets of terms, phrases, and clauses; the contrasts and
balances; sometimes the seesawing even—are at work, as we
should expect, in Burke's style. That was a hallmark of the

time, the movement of sober "eloquence" for better or worse. This structure in the sentences, however, while it serves in the *Letter* the end of sobriety, does not take possession of the reader and become fascinating for its own sake. It screens but does not enervate the feeling. In the following sentence, for example, charged as it is with such "warm" terms as *sullen, revenge, festers, rancor,* the periodic movement and the contrasts help to induce a sense of deliberation, of reasoning, and to suggest controlled intensity: "If your peace be nothing more than a sullen pause from arms, if their quiet be nothing but the meditation of revenge, where smitten pride smarting from its wounds festers into new rancor, neither the act of Henry the Eighth nor its handmaid of this reign will answer any wise end of policy or justice" (194). The balance stops short of see-saw by shifting syntax and avoiding a third *if* clause (if "smitten pride"), retaining the advantage of the basic rhythm.

Similar balances appear again and again in the movement of the *Letter.* "It would have been vain to oppose, and impossible to correct it" (200); "I cannot conscientiously support what is against my opinion, nor prudently contend with what I know is irresistible" (200).

These were considerations, Gentlemen, which led me early to think, that, in the comprehensive dominion which the Divine Providence had put into our hands, instead of troubling our understandings with speculations concerning the unity of empire and the identity or distinction of legislative powers, and inflaming our passions with the heat and pride of controversy, it was our duty, in all soberness, to conform our government to the character and circumstances of the several people who composed this mighty and strangely diversified mass (227).

"Our business was to rule, not wrangle; and it would have been a poor compensation that we had triumphed in a dispute, whilst we lost an empire" (227). "Our subjects diminish as our laws increase" (189).

That in the texture of the *Letter* which functions most generally, most continuously, and most pervasively to establish the reasonableness, the sense of restraint, the wisdom and soundness of both writer and message, is the moral and political aphorism (or *sentenia* in the familiar rhetorical and poetic sense). Burke's typical paragraph is focused and carried forward by one or more memorable generalizations of political principle or by shapely, incisive observations on the characteristic behavior of political and social man and his institutions. These generalizations are not doctrinal statements emanating from theoretical speculation. Rather are they notable, often pointed, distillations of common experience, illumining and enlarging particular circumstances into broad, deep contexts of human nature and historical experience. For example, Burke is destroying the fallacy that opposition to the Government in Parliament has exacerbated rebellion in America: "*General* rebellions and revolts of an whole people never were *encouraged*, now or at any time. They are always *provoked*"(217). This statement controls one of the strongest paragraphs on the subject, a paragraph which builds to that statement and evolves and derives its force from it. There is no need, I think, to reiterate illustration.

Burke's recent biographer Carl Cone remarks that in the *Letter:* "Characteristically, Burke asserted rather than proved his arguments, leaving it to his reader to react according to his instincts and emotions."[4] He should perhaps have gone on to observe that while trusting his readers to react according to their instincts and emotions, Burke so conducted the discourse that the instincts and emotions he touched were, as far as possible, those decent, honorable, humanitarian, commonsensical ones which Englishmen preferred to think themselves governed by. This he accomplished in various

[4] Carl B. Cone, *Burke and the Nature of Politics: The Age of the American Revolution* (Lexington, Ky.: University of Kentucky Press, 1957), 294.

ways, but persistently and cumulatively through forging page after page, conspicuous observations on socio-political morality and experience. He sought to sustain his position, he said, "by such arguments as may be supposed to have weight with a sober man" (197).

The rhetorical idiom of the *Letter to the Sheriffs of Bristol* is the idiom fitted to the "sober man," the sober man as reader ("audience") and the sober man as writer ("rhetor"). It is he whom the sensible, loyal, reasonable Englishman may be presumed to admire, to see personated in himself at his best, even when he is delighted with the polemic excursions of a *North Briton* or a *Junius*. It is he in whom is incarnated the "general sense of mankind." Throughout the *Letter*, as we have seen, Burke assumes that the sheriffs, his constituents, and the larger public whom he addresses are the "sober" men whom the writer himself exemplifies and with whom he seeks identification. They may need "strengthening, encouraging, or informing," and there may be things which "they either never have adverted to, or forgot in the rapid succession of the late unhappy Events."[5] They are always to be sharply distinguished, however, from the "violent men" (209–10) who are responsible for the calamitous state of the nation.

The sober man is stable, he is judicious, he is reasonable, but he is also capable of strong feeling, just passion, and "all possible energy" in the representation of things in their "true Colours."[6] He is capable of intense detestation of the brutalities of Hessian and Indian. He feels generous affection for "children" and kinsmen across the ocean. He nurtures abid-

---

[5] Burke to Richard Champion, his friend in Bristol, who was arranging publication of the *Letter* there, April 3, 1777, in Thomas W. Copeland (ed.), *Correspondence of Edmund Burke* (Cambridge, Eng.: Cambridge University Press; and Chicago: University of Chicago Press, 1958 ——), III, 333-34.

[6] *Ibid.*

ing love for English liberty and justice. That is the implied reader of the *Letter*, who is to be addressed not in polemic which cools from time to time into reasonableness, but in judicious indictment charged with honest warmth and rising often to powerful indignation. The sober man will prefer reason, equity, and the general sense of mankind to legal technicality, logic-chopping, and speculative philosophy. He trusts the old and tried and practical. Very near the beginning of the *Letter* Burke declares that "The old, cool-headed, general law is as good as any deviation dictated by present heat" (193), and he observes that "legislators ought to do what lawyers cannot; for they have no other rules to bind them but the great principles of reason and equity and the general sense of mankind" (196–97). "The general sense of mankind" serves repeatedly as a minor refrain to reinforce both Burke's indictment and his prescriptions for recovery. The sober man cherishes true liberty, but recognizes the practical restraints which must accompany and support it. "Liberty, if I understand it all, is a *general* principle, and the clear right of all subjects within the realm, or of none" (198). "Indeed, nothing is security to any individual but the common interest of all" (199). The sober man knows, but still may need to be reminded, that humanity has weaknesses which may prejudice its liberty, and that eternal vigilance is the price of freedom: "Parties are but too apt to forget their own future safety in their desire of sacrificing their enemies" (198); "The true danger is when liberty is nibbled away for expedients and by parts" (199); "It is by lying dormant a long time, or being first very rarely exercised, that arbitrary power steals upon a people" (201).

The factor in Burke's rhetorical composition which does most to control the tone and temper of the *Letter* is this felicitous generalization. Burke is not a notable "phrasemaker" or sloganeer in the present sense of those terms. His few catchy coinings have not been altogether happy, and he perhaps would have been pleased not to have written of the "swinish multitude." His faculty for producing memorable distillations of practical political wisdom, however, and felicitous general observations on the behavior of social man is obviously one of his notable resources as speaker and writer. It complements and is complemented by his tendency to "reason in metaphor." The impulse to concentrate "experience into manageable generalization," to lift toward generality, which W. J. Bate finds in Samuel Johnson,[7] produces the principal likeness between Burke's rhetorical style and his friend Johnson's.

All Burke's parliamentary speeches and political writings exhibit this generalizing characteristic, and from them, as from a rhetorico-political magazine, writers and speakers for two centuries have drawn reinforcement for discourse and have borrowed clinching statements for political argument.

"In other words, we are ... to consult our invention, and to reject our experience" (7). *On American Taxation*
"Refined policy ever has been the parent of confusion" (106). *On Conciliation*
"When bad men combine, the good must associate" (I, 526). *Present Discontents*
"Abstract liberty, like other mere abstractions, is not to be found" (120). *On Conciliation*
"An Englishman is the unfittest person on earth to argue another Englishman into slavery" (133). *On Conciliation*
"I do not know the method of drawing up an indictment against an whole people" (136). *On Conciliation*

---

[7] W. J. Bate, *The Achievement of Samuel Johnson* (New York: Oxford University Press, 1961), 29, 30.

"Crimes are the acts of individuals, and not of denomina-
tions" (418). *Speech at the Guildhall in Bristol*
"People will not look forward to posterity, who never look
backward to their ancestors" (III, 274). *Reflections on the
Revolution in France*

And so the gleaning could go on and has gone on, through the
speeches on the American War, economical reform, and India
to the *Reflections* and *A Letter to a Noble Lord*—the whole
corpus of Burke.

The part played by capsulated experience and aphoristic
wisdom varies in kind and quantity from circumstance to
circumstance. In evidential arguments, such as the parliamentary speeches on particular issues and propositions of
action, statements of those kinds appear less frequently. They
serve mainly to point up and elevate contentions. In the more
general and "philosophical" discourses such as the *Present
Discontents*, the *Letter to the Sheriffs*, and the *Reflections* they
serve more largely as vehicles of the argument.

As I have suggested, this aspect of Burke's rhetorical practice is especially prominent in the *Letter*. It may account in
considerable part for the high reputation which the *Letter* has
enjoyed among Burke's biographers and historians. Lord
Morley praised it, along with the speech-pamphlets *On American Taxation* and *On Conciliation*, as composing "the most
perfect manual in our literature, or in any literature, for one
who approaches the study of public affairs, whether for knowledge or for practice."[8] Lecky refers to it as Burke's "admirable
letter on the American question"[9]; Carl Cone sees it as "the
finest political disquisition Burke had produced since his

[8] John Morley, *Burke*, in English Men of Letters Series (London: Macmillan, 1882), 81.
[9] William Edward Hartpole Lecky, *A History of England in the Eighteenth
Century* (8 vols.; New York: D. Appleton, 1891), IV, 71.

Thoughts on the Present Discontents."[10] Various commentators choose different parts for special attention. Morley is attracted especially to the part of Burke's peroration in defense of morality in politics and government; Cone points to the "eloquent, generalized defense of pragmatism in government"; W. J. Bate sees in it "one of the classic pronouncements on political prudence and the imaginative use of fact"[11]; and the Burkean editors Hoffman and Levak choose to call it a "classic utterance on the necessity of prudence and avoidance of abstract theoretical extremes in the affairs of government."[12]

Burke, I think, induces these estimates through the same means which he applied to his contemporary public. The judicious reader with the perspective of a later day, unembroiled in the crises and passions of the American War and separated from the necessities of active contemporary debate, of course may discount the fears Burke seeks to arouse for the deterioration of English society and the destruction of English liberties. He may be wearied with Burke's insistent theme of the kinship of Englishmen in America and those at home. He may remind himself that the "Englishmen in the colonies" enlisted the "ferocious savages," when they could, against the redcoats and Hessians. He may be amused or bored at Burke's chauvinist distaste for Fort Knyphausen in the midst of English dominions; and if he be acclimated to the recent Namierite historical interpretations of the age of George III, he may well think Burke's indictment of North's policy and administration extravagant and wrongheaded; and he may be amazed

[10] Cone, *Burke and the Nature of Politics: The Age of the American Revolution,* 294.
[11] Walter J. Bate, *Edmund Burke: Select Works* (Modern Library ed.; New York: Random House, 1960), 12.
[12] Ross J. S. Hoffman and Paul Levack (eds.), *Burke's Politics: Select Writings and Speeches of Edmund Burke on Reform, Revolution, and War* (New York: Alfred Knopf, 1949), 96.

at Burke's wistful nostalgia for the "system" that prevailed before 1763.

Burke's cumulative sententious observations on human nature and politics, however, and not alone his more or less extended discussion of political prudence in the latter part of the *Letter*, serve, it seems, to produce in his commentators what such observations would obviously tend to produce in his immediate readers—the strong impression of "good sense [wisdom], good morals, and good will"[13] in the writer and soundness in the message. Planted in page after page of the text, they focus and intensify the meaning of passage after passage. Permeating the context, they tend to generate in a reader a sense of stability and of the reasonableness, the rightness, the necessity of Burke's indictment. Extracted and combined in coherent sequence, they might compose the sober man's credo of English liberty, the law, and prudent management of a wide and diverse empire.

Up to the last minute, and even between the publication of the Bristol and London editions, Burke was making changes in the text—to satisfy his stylistic sense and to anticipate criticism. On May 2, he wrote Champion, who was seeing to the printing in Bristol, that although the *Letter* was "written with much interruption," it would be "criticized in all probability much at leisure, and with much acrimony." He wished it, therefore, to "be as unexceptionable as such a thing can be." The changes he still wanted to make, if it were not too late, were "rather relative to clearing doubts than preventing objections."[14]

The *Letter* elicited the mixed response which was to be expected and which Burke anticipated. I have sampled (above,

---

[13] The classic ends of "ethical" proofs in the ancient rhetorical systems, particularly the Aristotelian.

[14] Copeland (ed.), *Correspondence*, III, 337–38.

pp. 109-10) the high opinions expressed by historians and biographers of later generations. One of the recent biographers, however, Sir Philip Magnus, is impressed chiefly by what he considers Burke's egregious fawning before his aristocratic colleagues.[15] Magnus is not alone in his judgment of Burke's general, public attitude and behavior toward the peers with whom he associated, but it suggests more the contemporary partisan than the judicious biographer. Horace Walpole, for example, a member of Opposition and a friend of America but no admirer of Burke, charged Burke with "sophistry, which was always tinged with monarchic and high ecclesiastic principles, and always reserved loopholes for displaying his real principles, if ever he should become a minister of the Crown"; and he sneered at the "laboured subterfuges and inconsistent Jesuitism of Burke."[16] The aged James Oglethorpe, founder of Georgia, volunteered a quite contrary response. On May 30 he wrote: "I did not dare tell you the Transports I felt in reading Your Letter to Bristol. That particular Paragraph, which Exhorts the Uniting honest Men in defense of Virtue, regardless of Parties, and Prejudices, is most Excellent, and I hope it will be followed. The Number of honest Men in England is Great, and their Influence much Greater, and I dare say they Rejoice to hear, that the Names you mention Join with you in saving the Kingdom, and us All from Destruction."[17]

For Burke a more gratifying response was doubtless that of the Scottish member of the Rockingham group, George Dempster, who wrote early in the summer: "I must embrace this opportunity likewise of thanking you for the pleasure which a second & third perusal of Your Letter to the Sherriffs

---

[15] Sir Philip Magnus, *Edmund Burke: A Life* (London: John Murray, 1939), 91–92.

[16] Steuart (ed.), *The Last Journals*, II.

[17] Copeland (ed.), *Correspondence*, III, 343–44.

[*sic*] of Bristol has afforded me. In manner it is highly classical & elegant & in matter most precious, being by much the best essay on the moderate practicable service of a free government I have ever read." Dempster finds that Burke has made ideas wonderfully clear which he "never expected to see so naturally & so well developed." "You also do great Honour & great Justice," he continues, "to that part of the Legislature with whom you have concurred in American measures." He mentions Burke's interpretation of "that System of which the repeal of the Stamp act made a striking part." Dempster enclosed a copy of a pamphlet sent him by the author, which Dempster playfully calls "an Antidote to the Poison which Your Letter contains." It was prepared, he thinks, before Burke's *Letter* appeared.[18]

Dempster's calling a portion of the Letter an "essay" on free government puts emphasis where Burke would have had a judicious reader put it; for, as I have shown, it enlarges from immediate controversy into lucid popular (though not simplistic) political philosophy, developed with the perspecuity which could please Dempster and enrage hostile readers. Sam Johnson, Burke's Tory friend, unlike Dempster, could approve of neither the "manner" nor the "matter!" Johnson "censured the composition much, and he ridiculed the definition of a free government . . . 'I will let the King of France govern me on those conditions, (said he,) for it is to be governed just as I please.' "[19] Johnson's lexicographical ridicule points up the hazard of definition separated from rhetorical context and function—of the quotable quotation, which comes easily to stand for the piece from which it is lifted.

The contemporary popular judgment of the *Letter* would

---

[18] Wentworth Woodhouse MSS at Sheffield City Library, Bk 655.
[19] 22 September 1777. *Boswell's Life of Johnson,* ed. by George Birkbeck Hill, revised and enlarged edition by L. F. Powell (6 vols.: Oxford: Clarendon Press, 1934), III, 186–87.

depend much more upon Burke's justification of the secession, especially of his absenting himself from debate on the *habeas corpus* bill, and on his pro-American, antiministerial sentiments than on exposition of prudential principles of government. The sympathizers with America would be hard to satisfy on the matter of *habeas corpus*, and the war party on his indictment of ministry. As he wrote to Champion, he had stayed away from the *habeas corpus* debate because he "did not like the Bill, nor any of the proposed or accepted amendments; and I should have the former to oppose against the Ministry, and the latter against a great part of the Minority."[20] And so had things turned out. Burke had cleared the ground for some and had pitted it further for others in a tortured area where he had much to lose by silence and doubtful immediate gains to make by speaking. The futility of "management" of opponents, however, and even of some of Opposition, cleared the way for the *Letter* to follow where the addresses had begun to lead—into a full and strong indictment-apologia which could undergird future behavior for him and his colleagues and show the war party in its "true Colours," without the inhibition necessary to a possible ascent to power. If the inconstancy of the Opposition in secession forced Burke into "sophistries" to justify his abstention on *habeas corpus*, the topics of indictment required no dubious rationalization, and the Burkean principles of prudential government, though they might be passed off as idealistic, could not but be admired by sober and virtuous men. True, Burke might temporize so as to displease the radical republicans on the "authority" of Parliament over the colonies, but within his and his party's principles he could move beyond even the second speech on conciliation to prefer—regretfully—"independency without war to independency with war." Burke's

---

[20] Copeland (ed.), *Correspondence*, III, 330.

early biographer (1798), the historian of George III, Robert Bisset, who wished to admire Burke but to maintain a judicious view of him, offers observations on the criticism of public controversy which should receive more consideration than sometimes they do in the judgment of rhetorical performances. Bisset thought the "celebrated" *Letter* one of Burke's "ablest performances," but he could see weaknesses in Burke's justification of his abstention on *habeas corpus*.

> Were we to consider the speech of an orator [he wrote, perhaps recalling Burke's passage on civil freedom] as we do the theorem of a mathematician, as stating a proposition either to be true or false, and by a chain of intermediations proving the asserted truth or falsehood; and to consider the speech as good or bad accordingly, as we should the demonstrations, many speeches of highest celebrity, the result of very great talents and knowledge, would be in no estimation.... We must often consider them rather as exhibitions of the general ability, knowledge, or feelings of the author, than as evictions of the truths undertaken to be proved.

That is, "rhetorical validity," as theorists from Aristotle on have understood, is not dependent upon apodeictic demonstration. If we estimate the excellence of Burke's *Letter*, Bisset continues, "by its fitness to justify his secession from parliament, his reasons do not amount to a justification. But although the state of the country, and the measures of government, even if they were as bad as Burke represents, do not prove that he was right in withdrawing his assistance, the letter is a fresh instance of his wonderful powers."[21]

Whatever Burke may have hoped for effects of the *Letter* in the enthusiasm of composing and launching it, he was soon inevitably aware that it had wrought no miracles in the ministry, the public at large, or the constituency at Bristol.

I was not without hopes [he wrote in August], that not only

[21] Robert Bisset, *The Life of Edmund Burke*... (London: George Cawthorn, 1798), 287–88, 282–84.

the taxes, but the many burthensome and vexatious circumstances that always attend new impositions, cooperating with the publick disgraces, and losses in Trade, would tend to put people extremely out of humour with those who have led them into War, with so very different promises both as to Conduct and as to Events. But I find that generally speaking they bear their Calamities, as they bear the Seasons; not as arising from the faults of those who rule them, but as dispositions of providence, at which they ought not to repine and are not able to oppose.[22]

Not until after the news arrived of Burgoyne's surrender, in late autumn, did there revive any hope in Burke and the Rockinghams for a turn in the public attitude.

The *Letter to the Sheriffs* was Burke's last major publication on the American problem, though that problem continued, at an even accelerated pace, to occupy his time, his energy, and his eloquence in the House of Commons, at least until his absorption in economical reform in 1779 and 1780. It is perhaps not farfetched to find in an early section of his *Speech at the Guildhall in Bristol* launching his brief election campaign of 1780, Burke's codicil to the *Letter* and his own implicit judgment of its significance. Explaining his absence from Bristol for the previous four years (one of the complaints circulated against him), he said that he could not bear to come before his constituents with the appearance of "I-told-you-so."

You remember [he said] that in the beginning of this American war (that era of calamity, disgrace, and downfall, an era which no feeling mind will ever mention without a tear for England) you were greatly divided,—and a very strong body, if not the strongest, opposed itself to the madness which every art and every power were employed to render popular, in order that the errors of the rulers might be lost in the general blindness of the nation. This opposition continued until after our great, but most unfortunate victory at Long Island.

[22] Copeland (ed.), *Correspondence*, III, 367. To Champion, 11 August 1777.

Then everything changed, and the "frenzy of the American war" overcame everything. The victory "perfected us in that spirit of domination which our unparalleled prosperity had but too long nurtured."

> We lost all measure between means and ends; and our headlong desires become our politics and our morals. All men who wished for peace, or retained any sentiments of moderation, were overborne or silenced; and this city was led by every artifice (and probably with more management because I was one of your members) to distinguish itself by its zeal for that fatal cause. In this temper of yours and of my mind, I should sooner have fled to the extremities of the earth than have shown myself here.

When circumstances changed and the "other face" of their calamity "showed itself in defeat and distress," he did not wish to have the least "appearance of insulting" them "with that show of superiority, which, though it may not be assumed, is generally suspected, in time of calamity, from those whose previous warnings have been despised." "But time," Burke concluded, "at length has made us all of one opinion, and we have all opened our eyes to the true nature of the American war,—to the true nature of all its successes and all its failures."[23] The *Letter to the Sheriffs of Bristol* had succeeded.

Burke's address to his constituents—and the nation—on the affairs of America, "made for the occasion of a day," did not "perish with it,"[24] as Burke had no intention that it should. Like the published *Speech on Conciliation* and the *Speech at the Guildhall,* it was eloquently made from a deep

---

[23] Burke, *Works* (1894), II, 375–76.

[24] In thanking William Robertson for a copy of his *History of America,* Burke wrote Robertson (10 June 1777) that he was sending him a "triffling temporary production, made for the occasion of a day, and to perish with it," in return for Robertson's "immortal work." Copeland (ed.), *Correspondence,* III, 352.

sense of the past, a detailed grasp of the present, and a sanguine view of the prospect of a future which sober men would wish for the English peoples. Arising upon the abandoned addresses to king and colonists, focusing powerfully the viable topics of indictment of ministry and war, and rising into fresh vindication of prudent, pragmatic government—and the good men who stood for it—against speculative politics and arbitrary power, the *Letter* was the fit and necessary rhetorical response to the exegencies of the critical situation of the man Edmund Burke was known to be as Member for Bristol, as ten-year parliamentary liberal, and as spokesman of a connection.

Like the *Present Discontents* and the *Speech on Conciliation,* it tipped no balance in prevailing politics or public sentiment; nor could it have done so, for there was no balance to tip. Events were too powerful to the contrary. It did not at once draw together a distracted and helpless minority. It did establish forcefully, however, the context and mood, if not the program of specifics, in which coalescence might come about; and it provided essential rhetorical remonstrance to the coercive force of jingoism, numbers, and repression. In the development of Burke's position in Parliament and his political views, the *Letter* is consolidating rather than innovative; but what is change of "front," in Morley's terms, rather change of "ground"[25] is often obscure in the context of fluid circumstances. Without a doubt, the *Letter* has been one of Burke's most admired if not best known performances. There is hardly a contrary voice among biographers and historians. Perhaps rhetoricians and students of public address and the literature of controversy might do well to look at it again. They might find it, even among the *Present Discontents,* the *Speech at the Guildhall* (1780), and the *Letter to a Noble Lord* (1796), Burke's prime achievement in the controlled fusion of indictment, personal apologia, and party manifesto.

[25] Morley, *Burke,* 169.

VI

A Concept of Eloquence

"Athens, the Eye of Greece, Mother of Arts
And Eloquence."

Thus in the last book of *Paradise Regained* (IV, 240)
does Milton's Satan bid Christ contemplate the highest
achievements of the pagan spirit—the arts, and Eloquence. So
has it been from the beginning—the Word, for better or for
worse. Sang the most poetic of the Apostles, "In the beginning
was the Word, and the Word was with God, and the Word was
God." "Him of the Western dome," wrote Dryden of the virtuous priest of David, "Him of the Western dome, whose weighty
sense/Flows in fit words and heavenly eloquence."[1] From the
beginning men have felt magic in eloquence—or divinity—
but in the semblance of eloquence, the voice of destruction.
But how tell the one from the other? That is the great problem.

The Voice—from Sinai or from Delphi—speaks with the
sanction of divinity. The talented human being, the inspired
genius, seems to borrow that sanction when he exhibits mastery of the Word and of the Event. We listeners may sense
mastery of the Word, and we may even be able to verify it by
acceptable indicators. Participation in the divinity, however,
we can only infer, and we may be deceived. Nevertheless,
throughout history eloquence, unlike rhetoric, has had a

[1] John Dryden, *Absalom and Achitophel*, I, 867–68.

pretty good reputation, if not always a thriving life.

What is eloquence? Here we go on yet another semantic safari! But let us take it by easy stages. The word *eloquence* may refer to anything in language from public speaking in general to the special hallmark of the divine afflatus. Sometimes eloquence is an attribute of a person, of an object, of an occasion; sometimes a quality of language, sometimes a genre of discourse. Historically and essentially, eloquence resides in speech and is public, but by extension and association it may be born and may thrive in almost any medium of expression and any occasion of communication. So John Donne can write,

> Her pure, and eloquent blood
> Spoke in her cheekes, and so distinctly wrought,
> That one might almost say, her body thought.[2]

And Sir Walter Raleigh: "Oh, eloquent, just, and mighty Death! whom none could advise thou has persuaded."[3] Or Wordsworth's: "One impulse from a vernal wood."[4]

Eloquence is great and good in the best of human intercourse, but it seems most conspicuously to be seen in the achievement of our forebears. It somehow appears as an adornment of a more golden age. It is most often the subject of interest and contemplation, apparently, in its decline, and it seems usually in decline—today, for example. Looking forward to the inundation of talk this election year, the *New Yorker* last January ruefully observed:

> It used to be that speechmaking was subject to a mysterious chemistry all its own. At best, if the right man spoke to the right audience at the right time and in the right

---

[2] John Donne, *Of the Progresse of the Soul*, "The Second Anniversary," 11. 244–46.
[3] Sir Walter Raleigh, *The History of the World* (1621), Bk. V, Ch. VI, the close.
[4] William Wordsworth, "The Tables Turned" (1798), l. 21.

place, he could do what Lincoln did at Gettysburg. At worst, the wrong man at the wrong time and in the wrong place could turn an audience, or a whole nation, into a mob, as Hitler did. But whatever this odd, invaluable, dangerous chemistry was, it has evaporated today. Political speeches are neither elevating nor demagogic; they are dead. Even when politicians take sharply opposing stands on issues, the quality of language and thought on both sides has a staleness that makes the charges and the counter-charges seem part of a single, colorless flow issuing from a common source. The mechanization of speechmaking has come close to destroying the point of making speeches. Taping and recording and the endless repetition of speeches have certainly destroyed any sense of occasion. Television, radio, and amplifiers may make the speaker available to a wider audience, but they also intervene between the speaker and his audience. And the speech-writers intervene between the speaker and his own thoughts. Too many people have got into the act. It seems most unlikely that we're going to find the right man at the right time in the right place between now and November 7th; it will be more a matter of nobody talking to no one about nothing.[5]

Sad and cynical—and evident—as that assessment and prognostic may seem, it is not special, though it is no doubt critical, to us in our time. "The quality of language and thought . . . has a staleness that makes charges and counter-charges seem part of a single, colorless flow issuing from a common source." That might have been spoken by a character in Tacitus' *Dialogue on Oratory* in the first century. "With the death of the Roman republic," wrote Harry Caplan, quoting from Secundus in that dialogue, " 'a hush fell upon eloquence.' " Significant public political speaking had no place in the state, the law courts receded to routine business, and even epideictic speaking—the funeral oration and panegyric—"enjoyed a history of progressive degradation for several centu-

---

[5] "The Talk of the Town; Notes and Comment," *New Yorker* (January 15, 1972), 19.

ries."[6] But decline is decline *from* something, decay is decay *of* something. The post-Alexandrine decline was the decay of Demosthenean "thunderbolt" to pyrotechnic rocket; the Roman, of Ciceronian "all-consuming conflagration" to theatrical illumination.

I have neither time nor competence to present even a capsulated history of the rise and fall of excellence in discourse. The perennial concepts of eloquence, however, interest me and I shall explore some of them briefly.

The prime concepts of eloquence through history, with variants of course, tend to be Longinian; or perhaps it is that the author of the ancient tractate on the "Sublime" came the nearest of all men to identifying the sources of a universal high experience from discourse. The Longinian doctrine embodies the late classical fusion of art and nature, of mind and spirit, of substance and form, of rhetoric and poetic, which sustains and legitimates the kinship of the literature of knowledge and the literature of power in the family of eloquence. That is, the principal and most common concepts of eloquence bring together natural genius, greatness or importance of idea and circumstance, power of mind or intellectual quality of thought, and special activity of imagination and emotion incarnated in fine and appropriate language.[7] That fusion of factors dominates, whether the critic attends mainly to the artist or to the artifact or even to the unembodied phenomenon.

What the revival of Longinus did of great importance for

---

[6] Harry Caplan, "The Decay of Eloquence at Rome in the First Century," in Anne King and Helen North (eds.), *Of Eloquence: Studies in Ancient and Mediaeval Rhetoric* (Ithaca, N.Y.: Cornell University Press, 1970), 160–61; reprinted from Herbert A. Wichelns *et al.* (eds.), *Studies in Speech and Drama in Honor of Alexander M. Drummond* (Ithaca: Cornell University Press, 1944), 295–325.

[7] Compare the five sources of elevation in language proposed in the Longinian tractate.

neoclassic criticism of the late seventeenth and the eighteenth centuries was to provide ancient authority and ancient genealogy for the sense of the inevitable limitation of art as a rationale for making or explaining works of human creativity. Such an art at its best can exercise salutary discipline over exuberant nature (genius), and from that art we learn its limits; we learn that nature alone is the source of the highest flights of creation. The imperfect masterpiece, therefore, is superior to the flawless product of art alone. Rhetoric may then be thought related to eloquence as poetic is to poetry. Poetry may "snatch a beauty beyond the reach of" poetics; and eloquence will rise to a power beyond the grasp of rhetoric.

Eloquence, variously but on the whole similarly defined in modern dictionaries, is etymologically related to elocution, both in the traditional rhetorical sense of the third of the five parts of rhetoric, *elocutio* (language, style), and in the sense developed in the eighteenth and nineteenth centuries of orality, delivery—the rhetorical *pronunciatio*. The primary definition in the *Oxford English Dictionary* is: "The action, practice, or art of expressing thought with fluency, force, and appropriateness, so as to appeal to the reason or move the passions— primarily of oral discourse, and hence applied to writing that has the characteristics of good oratory." The illustrative quotations from 1300 on down show that the basic meaning has remained about the same, though "in modern use the notion of *impassioned* utterance is more prominent than in the earlier example." In the *New International Dictionary* (2nd ed.) the principal definition is very like: "Discourse characterized by force and persuasiveness suggesting strong feeling or deep sincerity; esp. discourse marked by apt and fluent diction and imaginative fervor . . . — applied primarily to oral utterance." Each dictionary recognizes in third or fourth rank the common identification of eloquence with rhetoric, even as George

Campbell does in his great *Philosophy of Rhetoric*, where eloquence is the grand art by which discourse is adapted to its
end.

The great conscious lovers of eloquence, "l'éloquence," in
the modern world have been the French; and as we all know,
Frenchmen are sure that their language is more subtle and
at the same time more eloquent than any other—especially
the English and the German. From the seventeenth century
at least, eloquence has been associated in France very closely
with poetry, with literature, belles lettres. To René Rapin, for
example, eloquence is one of the four genres within belles
lettres, as examined in his major work, *Reflexions sur l'éloquence, la poétique, l'histoire et la philosophie* (1684). To Rapin *l'éloquence* seems to work as an attribute of nature,
commanding and delighting its audience through a fusion of
mind and emotion:

> Eloquence which touches only the understanding, the
> intellect, and doesn't get to the heart is not a true elo-
> quence. . . . Winding itself by imperceptible paths into the
> soul of those to whom it speaks, it makes such powerful
> impressions on them that they seem to respond less
> through judgment and counsel than by emotion and im-
> petuosity. All those beauties, therefore, which reach the
> intelligence without going to the heart are not genuine
> beauties.[8]

A few pages earlier Rapin had written: "Eloquence, which is
the true art of pleasing, never succeeds better at it than in
imitating nature. . . . The sovereign art of eloquence is to
attach itself scrupulously to nature as to its primary origin."[9]
Eloquence, therefore, is of the art that conceals art, the art
that is or appears spontaneous, that brushes away all sugges-

[8] Quoted by Hugh M. Davidson in *Audience, Words, and Art: Studies in
Seventeenth Century French Rhetoric* (Columbus: Ohio State University
Press, 1965), 53. Translation mine.
[9] *Ibid.*, 55 *n.* 6.

tions of calculation, of method, even of discipline, and strikes the hearer as instantaneous and spontaneous. It is the art of mind, soul, and passions at their strongest union in discourse.

Rapin seems to imply or assume the truth of beauty or the beauty of truth as fundamental to the power of eloquence. Bishop Fénelon demands truth explicitly. "I believe," he declares, "that all eloquence can be reduced to proving, to portraying, and to striking."[10] Beauty, yes, of course, but "I wish to know whether things are true before I find them beautiful."[11]

The close relation of oratory and poetry, which has clear origins in antiquity, is basic in the concept of eloquence for these Frenchmen and for their English contemporaries and successors. Discussing the portraying function of eloquence, the function, in Campbell's terms, of bringing to birth the "lively idea," Fénelon declares that "Poetry differs from simple eloquence only in this: that she paints with ecstasy with bolder strokes. . . . There is no eloquence at all without poetry."[12]

In the neoclassic frame of reference, where all art, especially poetry, is engaged in the service of instruction, it would be extraordinary if the grand art of persuasion should be sharply distinguished from the art of imaginative creation, and indeed it was not. In England, George Campbell considered poetry "no other than a particular mode or form of certain branches or oratory" comprehended under eloquence as "the grand art of communication not of ideas only, but of sentiments, passions, dispositions, and purposes."[13] Edmund

---

[10] Fénelon's *Dialogues on Eloquence*, translated with introduction and notes by Wilbur Samuel Howell (Princeton: Princeton University Press, 1951), "The Second Dialogue," 92.

[11] *Ibid.*, "The First Dialogue," 60.

[12] *Ibid.*, "The Second Dialogue," 93–94.

[13] George Campbell, *The Philosophy of Rhetoric* (7th ed.; London: Printed for William Baynes and Son, 1823), "Introduction," 7.

Burke, writing about Arthur Murphy's translation of Tacitus, relates poetry and oratory as modes of rhetoric sharing the quality of eloquence, but distinguished on the basis of their closeness to nature. Tacitus, says Burke, thinks deeply and paints strongly, "but he seldom or ever expresses himself naturally. . . . He did not write the language of good conversation. Cicero is much nearer to it." Tacitus and others, unhappily, aimed at a poetical style. "It is true," Burke goes on, "that eloquence in both modes or rhetorick is fundamentally the same; but the manner of handling is totally different, even where words and phrases may be transferred from the one of these departments of writing to the other."[14]

In the mid years of the eighteenth century in England, in the decades of Sir Robert Walpole just prior to the flowering of the oratory of Chatham, Burke, Fox, and their fellows in politics—in that age of "good sense" and gentlemanly taste in pulpit, courtroom, and Parliament, David Hume the philosopher and Oliver Goldsmith the gentle man of letters deplored a lack of eloquence in their contemporary Englishmen, and they wondered at it. Among the "polite and learned nations," says Hume, only England has a popular government or "admits into the legislature such numerous assemblies as can be supposed to lie under the dominion of eloquence."[15] But England has never produced, or at least never cherished, that sort of discourse. In the two houses of Parliament there are at least half-a-dozen speakers who are thought good, but they are high-grade journeymen—none is a master, none is eloquent. To Hume, as to many of the admirers of an eloquence which

[14] Thomas W. Copeland (ed.), *The Correspondence of Edmund Burke* (Cambridge and Chicago University Presses, 1968), VII, 502–503. Letter to Arthur Murphy, December 8, 1793.

[15] T. H. Green and T. H. Grose (eds.), *Essays Moral, Political, and Literary* (2 vols.; London: Longmans, 1875), I, 165.

they could not find about them in their own time, Demosthenes represented popular eloquence at its best, and Cicero was second only to him. "Could . . . [Demosthenes' quality of eloquence] be copied," Hume thought, "its success would be infallible over a modern assembly. It is rapid harmony, exactly adjusted to sense: It is vehement reasoning, without any appearance of art: It is disdain, anger, boldness, freedom, involved in a continued stream of argument." The passion of great ideas and of commitment to high causes, which Demosthénes embodied, is somehow deficient in modern Britain. The result, says Hume, is a kind of public address which is emotionally, spiritually unsatisfying. "Banish the pathetic from public discourses, and you reduce the speakers merely to modern eloquence; that is, to good sense delivered in proper expression."[16] Hume, of course, would not have a British eloquence offend taste by imitating the particular manners and cultural extravagances which pleased the ancients, but apparently he yearned, as our *New Yorker* critic does, for discourse to which he could succumb with excitement and delight and could contemplate afterwards with admiration. Had he recast his essay before he died, or had he lived out the eighteenth century of Chatham, Burke, Fox, Sheridan, Pitt, he might have allowed in them some near approximation to the eloquence which he admired in the ancients.

If Hume found English political eloquence especially lacking, Goldsmith took as dim a view of the bland dullness of the pulpit, especially of preaching to the ordinary folk. The "vulgar," he said, do not need rational theology but passionate exhortation. Though the Methodist preachers are ignorant, not bred and educated as gentlemen, he is forced to observe "how often and how justly they affect their hearers." "Did our

---

[16] *Ibid.*, I, 169, 170.

bishops . . . testify the same fervour, and *entreat* their hearers, as well as *argue*, what might not be the consequence!" Eloquence is lacking: the discourse that "elevates the Mind." "*A man . . . may be called eloquent, who transfers the passion or sentiment with which he is moved himself, into the breast of another.*"[17]

Both Hume and Goldsmith assume that eloquence is by nature oral and spontaneous, or spontaneous-seeming—that the extemporaneous is the only mode free enough to accommodate it. But the spontaneous overflow must be the overflow of a great and ready store of mind and passions. The most uninhibited presentation of that concept comes in the next century from Germany, another place and time when oratory (*Beredsamkeit*) was in decay and eloquence, it seems, could be found only abroad. In 1812, Adam Müller, the friend of Heinrich Gentz and disciple of Edmund Burke, published his *Twelve Essays on Eloquence and its Decay in Germany*. In the sixth essay, "On Political Eloquence and its Decay in Germany," Müller makes a panegyric to spontaneity and orality, which he illustrates from Fox and Burke in their great quarrel and separation on the floor of the House of Commons[18] over the French Revolution:

> A god speaks through the mouth of man when man really *speaks*. And the god should certainly not wait for his listeners, but these must be present first, then he appears. That is the spell of that unintentional eloquence, which a great moment itself brings about. A few disconnected words can produce effects which intentional eloquence never reaches, because they fall squarely into the present and because they are precisely suited to the disposition of the orator and

[17] Oliver Goldsmith, *The Bee*, No. VII (Saturday, November 17, 1759), "Of Eloquence." In *The Bee and Other Essays of Oliver Goldsmith, Together with the Life of Beau Nash* (Oxford Edition; London: Oxford University Press, 1914), 68–77.

[18] Debate on the Bill for the Government of Quebec. The passionate separation came to a climax on the night of May 11, 1791. See *Parliamentary History*, XXIX, 364-430.

his assembly toward each other, as also to the occasion and the state of mind.[19]

The immediacy of the eloquence of oratory, its dependence upon the particular situation, its incarnation in orality, in the voice and person of the speaker and the ear and person of the listener—for Müller this immediacy distinguishes eloquence from poetry.

> The real miracle of eloquence [he says] is only for the enviable ones present. And even if all words of that night [of the Burke-Fox parting] had been left behind for us, who can reproduce the *tones*? This is the advantage of the poet! Duration compensates him for all sufferings . . . for being deprived of the present actual glory. A speech . . . without its author . . . is nothing; it is not independent, not released by its author, not emancipated, not declared to be free as a work of poetry.[20]

Though each reading or recitation of a poem is, of course, a recreation, a poem is so created that the person, the physical voice of the poet is not a significant element. Orations too may be recreated, reenacted, but each is a different rhetorical work —not a version of an original.

The distinctiveness which face-to-face orality generates in eloquence, and the implication of orality for the relation of rhetorical discourse with literature have been skillfully and imaginatively explored and philosophically explicated by Carroll C. Arnold in a piece in *Philosophy and Rhetoric* under the title "Oral Rhetoric, Rhetoric, and Literature."[21] It is a fine scholarly statement, some of whose implications reinforce the lyrical presentation by Müller.

---

[19] *Zwölf Reden über die Beredsamkeit und deren Verfall in Deutschland,* mit einem Essay und einem Nachwort von Walter Jens (Frankfort: Insel Verlag, 1967), 114–15. I take the English with thanks from Dennis Bormann's forthcoming translation of the *Zwölf Reden.*

[20] *Ibid.,* 109.

[21] Carroll C. Arnold, "Oral Rhetoric, Rhetoric, and Literature," *Philosophy and Rhetoric,* I, 4 (Fall, 1968), 191-210.

We have seen Fénelon, Campbell, and Burke identifying poetry and eloquence in the realm of belles lettres. Later writers, perhaps under the influence of the Romantic shift in the ideas of poetry, have used the concept of eloquence to establish a distinction in mode or function instead of an identity. So for John Stuart Mill the difference between the literary and the rhetorical lies in this, that "Eloquence is written to be heard, poetry to be overheard." When the poet, says Mill, "turns round and addresses himself to another person; when the act of utterance is not in itself the end, but a means to an end—viz. by the feeling he himself expresses, to work upon the feelings, or upon the belief, or the will, of another,—when the expression of his emotions, or of his thoughts tinged by his emotions, is tinged also by that purpose, by that desire of making an impression upon another mind, then it ceases to be poetry, and becomes eloquence."[22]

Here is the familiar "intentional" or "instrumental" distinction again—this time concerning "thoughts tinged by . . . emotions," the substance of both poetry and eloquence. Another view, that of the American literary naturalist John Burroughs, exploits the distinction reminiscent of that between Edmund Burke's *sublime* and his *beautiful;* that between the delicate and the strong, the quiet and the loud, the finer and the more gross, calmness and excitement. Poetry begins, says Burroughs, "where eloquence ends; it is higher and finer harmony. Nearly all men feel the power of eloquence, but poetry does not sway the multitude; it does not sway at all,—it lifts, and illuminates, and soothes. . . . Eloquence is much more palpable, real, available. . . . Eloquence is a torrent, a tempest, a mass in motion, an army with banners, the burst of a hundred instruments of music."[23] Bur-

[22] J. W. M. Gibbs (ed.), *Early Essays of John Stuart Mill* (Bohn's Standard Library; London: Bell, 1897), 209.

[23] *Literary Values and Other Papers,* Volume X of *The Writings of John*

roughs associates eloquence with the martial, with "action," with the shaping of events. "It takes captive the reason and understanding. Its basis is earnestness, vehemence, depth of conviction. There is no eloquence without heat, and no poetry without light. . . . Eloquence belongs to the world of actual affairs and events." And so Burroughs goes on in an ecstasy of comparison from which it is easy to derive the impression that he knows he should cherish poetry but he really loves eloquence.

There is no conspicuous virtue without its corresponding vice, no great venture without its consequent hazard, and no high ornament of the human spirit without its hollow or gaudy imitation. Hence, of course, sham eloquence has drawn the contempt of the wise through the ages, and good sense has been preferred to fine language if we can't have them fused into one. Wrote Bacon, "Discretion of speech is more than eloquence; and to speak agreeably to him with whom we deal is more than to speak in good words and good order" (*Of Discourse*). "He that can carp in the most eloquent or acute manner at the weakness of the human mind is held by his fellows as almost divine," sneered Spinoza.[24] And many an honest academic will concur in the characteristic Thoreauism, "What is called eloquence in the forum is commonly found to be rhetoric in the study."[25] More of that later, perhaps, but we may commend Thoreau for his skill in abusing two of our favorite concepts in one brief sentence!

The nineteenth century in America was as gluttonous for public discourse and as proud of the eloquence of its spoke-

Burroughs (23 vols.; Boston and New York: Houghton-Mifflin, 1904–1923), Chapter VIII, "Poetry and Eloquence," 177–84.

[24] Benedict Spinoza, *Ethics*, Part III, Preface.

[25] Henry David Thoreau, "Reading," in *Walden, The Writings of Henry David Thoreau* (20 vols.; Cambridge: Riverside Press, 1906), II, 113.

men, its great leaders in senate, platform, and pulpit, as any age and nation has ever been; but it was also sensitive to the hazards of the false and pretentious and to the inadequacies of the limited. To Emerson, who composed at least two lecture-essays on eloquence:

> It is not powers of speech that we primarily consider under this word Eloquence, but the power that, being present, gives them their perfection, and, being absent, leaves them a merely superficial value. Eloquence is the appropriate organ of the highest personal energy. Personal ascendency may exist with or without adequate talent for its expression. . . . But when it is weaponed with a power of speech, it seems first to become truly human, works actively in all directions, and supplies the imagination with fine materials.[26]

Even Emerson, of course, could be realistic at times, if not doubtful: "One of our statesmen said, 'The curse of this country is eloquent men.' And one cannot wonder at the uneasiness sometimes manifested by trained statesmen, with large experience in public affairs, when they observe the disproportionate advantage suddenly given to oratory over the most solid and accumulated public service."[27] The adulatory vein, however, dominates Emerson's portrait of the eloquent man: "His mind has some new principle of order. Where he looks, all things fly into their places. . . . By applying the habits of a higher style of thought to common affairs of this world, he

[26] Ralph Waldo Emerson, "Eloquence," *The Works of Ralph Waldo Emerson* (5 vols.; New York: Bigelow, [192–?]), III, 261.

[27] *Ibid.*, III, 256–57. The sentiment in this passage, the eternally Platonic, appears in as uninhibited a form as one could wish in a work which Emerson could have known, the *De l'Eloquence* of the disillusioned French revolutionary, Joseph-Marie Lequinio. Lequinio idealized the rational in modern, civilized man, which he saw subverted all around him by what passed for eloquence: "What is eloquence? The art of fooling men and making them like their error, a sure means for schemes to succeed, and the scourge of liberty." Translated by Stafford Thomas, "A Terrorist's Rhetoric: Citizen Lequinio's 'De l'Eloquence'," *Speech Monographs*, XXXIX (1972), 51–52.

introduces beauty and magnificence wherever he goes." "The truly eloquent man," he declares again, "is a sane man with the power to communicate his sanity."[28]

Daniel Webster, incarnate eloquence, saw eloquence as the great manifestation of the godlike in man, inaccessible to art and study alone. In his eulogy of Adams and Jefferson he said:

> When public bodies are to be addressed on momentous occasions, when great interests are at stake, and strong passions excited, nothing is valuable in speech farther than it is connected with high intellectual and moral endowments. Clearness, force, and earnestness are the qualities which produce conviction. True eloquence, indeed, does not consist in speech. It cannot be brought from far. Labor and learning may toil for it, but they will toil in vain. . . . It must exist in the man, in the subject, and in the occasion. . . . It comes, if it come at all, like the outbreaking of a fountain from the earth, or the bursting forth of volcanic fires, with spontaneous, original, native force. . . . The clear conception outrunning the deductions of logic, the high purpose, the firm resolve, the dauntless spirit, speaking on the tongue, beaming from the eye, informing every feature, and urging the whole man onward, right onward to his object—this, this is eloquence; or rather it is something greater and higher than all eloquence, it is action, noble, sublime, godlike action.[29]

Eloquence is of man, of an individual man speaking for his fellows and with them in their moments of hard decision.

In a measure to summarize or crystallize this very selective historical sketch of the concept of eloquence, I return to France and to the *Larousse du XXe siècle*.[30] The *Larousse* entry for "Eloquence" defines it as "the natural talent for

[28] Emerson, *Works*, III, 266, 267.

[29] The text of this passage is available in many sources. See, for example, David Brewer, *The World's Best Orations* (St. Louis: Kaiser, 1899), X, 3852.

[30] Translations mine.

persuasion ... [which] must not be confounded with rhetoric, which is the art of speaking well. Even though Quintilian said, 'One is born a poet, one becomes an orator,' eloquence is a gift and can exist independently of any education and study." Eloquence in the pulpit, and to a lesser extent at the bar, has appeared, the *Larousse* writer agrees, throughout postclassical history, and France can boast of distinction in both. "Political eloquence," however, "extinguished since the last days of the Roman republic, had shot up only rare lights like Rienzi and Savanarola until the birth of the English Parliament. It was in England that political eloquence was born anew with Chatham, his son William Pitt, Fox, Burke, O'Connell, Robert Peel, Lord Russell, Lord Derby, Disraeli, Gladstone, etc." In France, the encyclopedist finds, political eloquence appeared with the Revolution in such as Mirabeau, Maury, Danton, "and almost all the Girondins"; but *Larousse du XXe siècle* failed to discover America.

The fusion in discourse of truth and beauty, of idea and feeling, of thought and imagination in the service of idea and action—that is the concept of eloquence overriding particular fashions and particular rhetorical customs. So, for example, J. H. C. Grierson called Burke's "an eloquence in which the wisdom of his thought and the felicity of his language and imagery seem inseparable from one another."[31] The *Times* called Fox's Reform speech of 1797 (May 29) "a *chef d'oeuvre* of eloquence, of sound reasoning and mature reflection." To Edward Channing in the nineteenth century, "Modern eloquence," aimed "at making men think patiently and earnestly; it has only to secure a lodgment for truth in the mind, and then by and by the truth will quietly prevail."[32] And Sir

---

[31] *Cambridge History of English Literature* (1914), XI, 8.
[32] Edward Channing, "The Orator and his Times," Dorothy I. Anderson and Waldo W. Braden (eds.), *Lectures* (Carbondale, Ill.: Southern Illinois University Press, 1968), 19.

Herbert Read, the literary scholar and critic of this century: "Eloquence . . . is the art of exposition animated by an intuitive grasp of the greatness of its theme."[33] "True eloquence," he says, incorporating a phrase from Bolingbroke, "is intuitive in its nature, and is 'fed by an abundant spring.' It flows when some dominant idea has mastery of the mind and orders the expression to the single purpose of that idea. Everything, every subordination and subtlety of style, is driven into one persuasive unity."[34] "Eloquence may inhere in a phrase . . . but the two first-named conditions of eloquence—an adequate theme and a sincere and impassioned mind—really imply a mood that is sustained within the extent of the subject. An adequate theme, like victory, courage, beauty, God, nature, or the infinity of space, cannot be confined to a few paltry phrases, but creates a mood of expansive fury."[35] And so, from the history of the concepts of eloquence, embodying as they do interfusion of the poetic and the rhetorical, I choose to see within the rhetorical the high ground on which literature and philosophy share Plato and Bacon and Rousseau and Hume and Kierkegaard and Camus and Sartre; on which literature and politics share Swift and Burke and Lincoln and Milton and the *Federalist* and Disraeli. And for this high common ground there is plenty of historical precedent for the name and concept *eloquence*.

I have explored this concept modestly in another place,[36] where I suggested that in many areas of public discourse, the man of literary experience, of poetic imagination—the Burke, the Disraeli, the Churchill (to use Stephen Graubard's as-

[33] Sir Herbert Read, *English Prose Style* (2nd ed.; Boston: Beacon Press, 1952), 167.
[34] *Ibid.*, 171.
[35] *Ibid.*, 175.
[36] Donald C. Bryant, "Uses of Rhetoric in Criticism," in Donald C. Bryant (ed.), *Papers in Rhetoric and Poetic* (Iowa City: University of Iowa Press, 1965), 13.

sociation)[37] or the Cicero—extends political thought in a dynamic dimension which is not to be derived from the philosopher and the theorist on the one hand or the man of affairs on the other. I will not take the time to review that exploration, but I will extend it in a brief example.

If there has been public eloquence in the twentieth century, there would be little dissent to the proposition that Winston Churchill exemplified it; and if political oratory may still be literature, perhaps we might agree that at his best and almost by nature Churchill spoke something close to literature when the impulse of an occasion roused him to the magnitude of his language, to the seriousness of the situation or importance of the issue, to the power of his images, to the dynamic movement of the rhythm of his sentences, to the majesty of his voice and utterance. Passages from his speeches on grand occasions echo in the minds of growing generations, like passages from Lincoln and from Kennedy's inaugural address (though Kennedy and Churchill have not receded far enough yet into history to be immune to the carpings of cynical reaction).

To advance the notion I wish to promote at this point, I will examine, not one of Churchill's famous masterpieces, but his performance on an occasion short of grand, though in a measure splendid nevertheless, when the touch of literature seemed to descend upon a Churchillian passage.

I am thinking of a speech which I heard him make to the foregathered steel magnates of Sheffield at the Master Cutler's Feast in 1951. Though already technically nationalized, steel was actually free. At any moment, however, the Labor Government might feel secure enough to move in and supersede the magnates of the Master Cutler's Society.

---

[37] Stephen Graubard, *Burke, Disraeli, and Churchill: The Politics of Perseverence* (Cambridge, Mass: Harvard University Press, 1961).

At best the speech was topical, for Churchill more or less routine, and he met the occasion without inflating it. The main idea came to life in an image which not only delineated the situation of the industry as Tory Churchill conceived it but *created* his conception in the setting for the audience. He envisioned the vulture of socialism, the scavenger bird of prey, circling and drifting expectantly, hungrily, above the furnaces and yards of Sheffield Steel—slowly, grimly, ponderously, even as he developed the image. The bird, he implied, would finally drop—exhausted and unfed.

Theatrical corn? No doubt. But so is Richard's "A horse, a horse!" out of context and in print. I cite the image because it is born in ordinary circumstances and might be thought by a reader (or a cynic in the audience) an ordinary oratorical stereotype from the repertory of pseudo-meaning. It is therefore a fair example of what the Thoreaus of this world contemn as the eloquence of the forum turned to the rhetoric of the study. It could have been a fraud, but it wasn't. For those who heard it, it effected the fusion of speaker, delivery, matter-at-issue, language, image, occasion, and audience into a live articulation of meaning—into a commanding moment of eloquence.[38]

Let us in conclusion return briefly to the Thoreauvian aphorism, for in a way it reflects a kind of common experience; and, of more importance, it characterizes certain sorts of men of letters who tend to be chary of the oral dimension of mean-

[38] I heard the speech from the press table in the wings, April 17, 1951. A text is printed in Winston S. Churchill, *Stemming the Tide: Speeches 1951–1952*, ed. Randolph S. Churchill (London: Cassell, 1953), 45–47. The two sentences suggesting the image of the vulture come two-thirds of the way through the speech: "The Steel Corporation vulture hovers in the sky with its two grasping claws, Uniformity and Monopoly. It has not dared to swoop and its life may be short." That the image made the speech is corroborated by another who heard it, and by the headline on the brief story in the *Times* the next day (p. 4, col. 6): "STEEL CORPORATION VULTURE." The story begins with the two sentences in question.

ing, or at least the public oral dimension—especially that contributed (they would say, imposed) by the orator, but even by the actor. Perhaps we may ask why the appearance of discourse in the study should be categorically assumed truer and more just than its appearance in the forum? Shall we not render unto the study the things that are the study's, and unto the forum the things that belong there? Shall we take it as a principle of criticism that discourse is better judged in its incomplete or defective form than in its full and complete embodiment? It is to be assumed as a critical principle that the dimension of meaning generated in the live public confrontation or identification is a false or illegitimate dimension, to be burnt away by the study lamp, so that the honest meaning may survive in the ashes? Are we to believe that the Fénelons and the Müllers, the Humes and the Arnolds, have been the dupes and only the Thoreaus and Lequinios can be trusted? Of course not, you reply, when put that way! But still, you protest, isn't it easier to deceive people through their ears than their eyes? Perhaps—some people by some speakers sometimes. Isn't it easier also to enlighten and inspire those same people through oral discourse than through print?

I am certainly not proposing that real eloquence is oral and that versions in print are fakes. Far from it. Almost all the characteristics and effects of eloquence which we have reviewed may be exhibited and generated by written discourse and by oral. The means, however, are not the same, any more than they are between the *Forsyte Saga* and the BBC-TV dramatization. There is obviously a living eloquence of the moment, of the responsive situation-speaker-hearer-speaker-situation, which can be generated even by fragments of words and by signs, or by strategic silence. This is the kind sometimes coveted by such as our *New Yorker* critic, and more often the kind that is feared. It is the kind that may become desiccated or false in print, for it grows from active participation in a self-generating audiovisual event. Wimsatt's concept of style as creating the ultimate refinement of meaning is a just concept, making form a part of substance.[39] It is a proper, an essential concept for guiding criticism of oral discourse, for delivery must be assumed a dimension of style.

The eloquence of the pen works through means of animating language different from those of the eloquence of orality, even as poetry does. The setting must be brought into being by the *reader*, from the image-inducing and the chord-touching potential of print alone. The eye-language, converted to speech-like sounds and rhythms from the reader's learned sensitivities and accustomed associations, forces him to create in imagination a speaker through whom and with whom he responds to the fusion of literature and idea-in-action.

That speeches read well, or read ill, silently and in print, neither degrades oral performance nor authenticates eloquence. The greater the dimension which *body* and *sound,* acting on circumstance and setting and responding to them, create in the total rhetorical transaction, the more defective or incomplete is the merely verbal text of eloquent discourse. How much less is the dead body of Churchill on the catafalque in Westminster than the living orator on the dais in Master Cutler's Hall! The greater the dimension which *structure* and *style* create in the rhetorical transaction, the more nearly may the eloquence of print equal or exceed that of voice.

A concept of eloquence, in sum, I find serviceable to characterize that mixed kind of discourse whose worth arises partly from contemplation or experience and enjoyment, and partly from use. The eloquent lies thus between the pure poetic and the pure rhetorical and participates in both; and I am satisfied to conclude on that note, for "To disparage eloquence," wrote

---

[39] W. K. Wimsatt, Jr., *The Prose Style of Samuel Johnson* (New Haven: Yale University Press, 1941), 11, 63.

John Morley in his *Life of Gladstone*, "is to depreciate mankind."[40] To study eloquence is to travel one of the principal thoroughfares of the advancement of the human spirit.

[40] John Morley, *Life of Gladstone* (New ed.; New York, 1932), II, 594.

Index